TurnAround Schools

Creating Cultures of
Universal Achievement

Jeff King and Damen Lopez

DEDICATION

This book is dedicated to the Los Peñasquitos Elementary School staff. These wonderful people have collectively created an extraordinary elementary school that knows no limits to the academic success of every student.

Los Peñasquitos staff members come to work every morning and look into the eyes of remarkable children, many of whom struggle because of generational poverty and the challenges of learning English. They don't see broken children who have little hope; they see only young people with the ability to work hard and be responsible, and with the potential to be academically successful and ultimately prepared to attend college.

These educators believe in their own potential to make a difference. They focus solely on strategies that positively impact student learning. They never give up and they never make excuses. And they smile — every day and all day.

Thank you, each of you. You inspire us.

CONTENTS

Chapter 8

PREFACE

Damen Lopez spent his childhood living with his family in a room above a country store and eating food purchased with government assistance. Jeff King moved as a teenager from a small segregated town in California to his new home in Tanzania, East Africa, learning for the first time that people of all colors can be loyal friends, good neighbors, and equal contributors to society.

Eventually, the two of us became partners in the most noble of ventures — advocating for the academic success of children who otherwise would have had little hope. Our childhood experiences inspired our commitment to confront a broken system and dare public elementary schools to demand that their most disenfranchised children rise above their challenges and courageously pursue the dream of a college education.

Like Martin Luther King Jr., we have been to the mountain, and we looked over and saw the Promised Land. The Promised Land we saw was elementary schools, dozens of elementary schools across America, where children of color, children who are learning English, children who endure the scourge of generational poverty, beat academic odds and successfully prepare themselves to attend college.

These schools are modern day educational miracles, but what they do is not magic. Our message is that their successes can also be yours. Our hope is that they will.

C H A P T E R

1

"Today the Revolution Begins!"

It is not the mountain we conquer, but ourselves.

Sir Edmund Hillary

"You don't believe all your students can learn." In 1997 these simple words began a learning revolution that is spreading across America.

At that time, Los Peñasquitos Elementary School (in San Diego, California) was like many of today's elementary schools. It was a happy place, but its low-income students struggled to be academically successful. Los Pen, as the school is affectionately called, was the lowest performing elementary school in the Poway Unified School District, and it had been for the previous twenty-six years. Everyone knew that most of its poor kids did not achieve well, and very few people expected anything different.

Why did most people accept the dismal achievement of those many Los Peñasquitos students? You've heard the reasons yourself. After all, many of the students at Los Peñasquitos were *those* kids. You know. Those kids spoke thirty-five languages. Those kids lived in federally subsidized housing

3

across from the school. Those kids were brown and black which made it convenient for some to make excuses. Many of those kids came from homes where parents had little interest in their education, neglect was frequent, and two-parent families were rare. Those kids were easy to love but tough to teach.

On an August morning in 1997, two days before the children returned to school, Jeff King, the new principal, and his staff gathered in the cafeteria for the annual event all elementary teachers know so well — the welcome back meeting. The arrival of a new principal always creates an air of anticipation, and the tone of the meeting was friendly and polite. The staff sat in folding metal chairs arranged in three semi-circles, and that morning the always-delicate relationship between staff and principal began to form. At the end of the agenda, the new principal took a deep breath and said, "Now, I want to tell you something about you. Actually, I want to tell you two things. Can I do that?"

What could they say except, "Sure"?

"First, you are some of the hardest working, kindest, most loving people I've ever met. That's the truth. Every day you come to school and shower your students with love and compassion, and they appreciate that more than you will ever know." The staff members smiled because it's always great to hear something nice about yourself, especially when those words are true.

"And there's something else I want to tell you about you. You don't believe all your students can learn."

Those simple words hit like a bombshell. The room was hushed. No one had ever spoken the truth before. After an uncomfortable silence, Karon, one of the most respected teachers on staff, raised her hand and said, "Jeff, you've been here for exactly one hour. Some of us have taught here for twenty-six years. How can you say we don't believe all our students can learn?"

"Karon, I can say that because they don't." He continued, "I know these kids come with all sorts of challenges, but if you believed they could learn, they would. They're not stupid. Somehow over the years, if you truly believed in their potential, you would have figured out different ways to make it happen."

"But yesterday is yesterday, and today is today. From this moment on, we're going to expect that every student will be academically successful, even those kids who are the toughest to teach. And we won't just expect them to learn. You and I are going to figure out together how to make that happen."

"Understand this — I don't have a clue how we're going to do it. And neither do you. But together we'll work, and work, and continue to work to find answers where no answers exist. Every day we'll get better at educating these deserving students. We're the only hope many of them have. Today, the revolution begins!"

Imagine the conversations that must have taken place later that day in the parking lot. But those good teachers soon agreed that the moral imperative for educating their most difficult learners was just too great. With a collective courage not previously seen at that school, those teachers agreed to work together to achieve academic excellence for every child.

It helped that their principal promised to be their biggest cheerleader, supporting them in their successes and failures and protecting them from petty people inside and outside the district who felt it was their duty to quietly sabotage the work of creative teachers who dared to step outside the box. Together, the staff made the bold decision to flout conventional thinking, roll up their sleeves, and begin the exhilarating and sometimes exhausting journey that eventually resulted in a school that knows no limits to the academic achievement of its students.

Los Peñasquitos no longer languishes at the bottom of the district, and the future is now very different for disadvantaged children who call Los Peñasquitos home. The turnaround has been stunning. Even though the demographics of Los Peñasquitos are largely unchanged, its children now perform among the top ten percent of students throughout California. Furthermore, in both 2006 and 2007, when compared to one hundred similar California elementary schools, Los Peñasquitos Elementary School was number one. This is important only because it means that many Los Peñasquitos students will now be the first in their families to attend college, leave behind lives of poverty, and have a fighting chance to grasp the American dream.

It has been twelve years since that August welcome-back meeting, and many people proudly look back to that morning as the moment that began the learning revolution at Los Peñasquitos Elementary School.

THE REVOLUTION

Our country is on the brink of a revolution. The battle cry of the revolution is this:

Poor children can learn! Minority children can learn! Children who have not yet mastered English can learn! Outstanding educators at every elementary school in America hold the keys for making that academic success a reality.

These are radical statements. Few people publicly disagree that all elementary school children can learn. To do so would be politically incorrect. But many also hedge their bets with a series of ifs: if the children have supportive parents, if they eat a good breakfast, if they arrive to school on time, if they speak English, if they are well behaved, if their families avoid the influences of gangs and drugs and violence — if, if, if. What begins as an acknowledgement of the potential of all children often ends with excuses as to why that potential can't be realized.

It is the job of most elementary educators to work every day with children who have all sorts of challenges. Their children may speak English as a second language and come from humble immigrant families. They often live in housing projects and witness more than their fair share of crime and violence. These children experience all the social distractions commonly associated with poverty, and these experiences make teaching difficult and learning a challenge. Yet there is hope.

Across this nation and in almost every state, elementary schools that are sanctuaries of academic excellence exist in the most unpredictable and surprising places — often bleak urban areas where many children grow up having little hope of a life beyond the streets. But the remarkable truth is that these exceptional elementary schools are filled with students who proudly defy the expectations of a cynical society. Because of media portrayals of inner city schools, visitors often enter these sanctuaries of academic excellence expecting to meet academically comatose children and defeated teachers vainly attempting to maintain order. But these visitors are stunned to encounter students who are respectful and happy, classrooms that are orderly, teachers who are competent, loving, and committed, and data that prove these children are as academically successful as their more affluent peers.

Many of us have been led to believe that poverty causes academic mediocrity or worse. That is a lie. It is true that poverty creates issues that make teaching and learning more difficult. Poverty places a tremendous responsibility on schools to ensure the academic success of all students. But poor children, as a group, are not stupid. They deserve the best, and they often want the best. At many schools across America, these children are proving to a skeptical society that they are just as academically capable as their affluent friends who live on the other side of town.

Here is the most important point of this book: If one school, and another, and another, have successfully discovered strategies that enable all groups of children to be successful, even those children who are the most difficult to teach, then it can be done. The question is no longer what or why or even how, but rather will you and your school also embrace the strategies that make this learning revolution possible?

The Plan is Simple, the Work is Difficult

It is commonly accepted that the challenge of educating disadvantaged children is so complex, with tentacles of responsibility reaching into so many crevices of society, that this noble ideal is all but unachievable. Who can blame those who have thrown up their arms in defeat? The many negative effects of poverty on families and communities are undeniable. Children living in these circumstances inevitably bring related challenges into their classrooms every day, frustrating the children, their teachers, and the broader system. Can teachers and administrators solve the pervasive societal problems their students face? The practical answer is no, at least not in the short term.

We have worked in this world for many years, and confess that at times we fell victim to the same seemingly practical, but defeatist thinking. But we continued to hear a small voice that asked, "If these problems are so difficult to solve, why is it that students at some low-income schools (perhaps only a few) are so surprisingly successful? What do these schools do differently? Can their successes be replicated by other public elementary schools?" We found answers to those questions that should bring hope to every elementary school educator who has ever said, "I would do whatever it takes to help my students accomplish their dreams, if only I knew what to do."

As we learned about low-income elementary schools where children beat the academic odds, we were taken aback by the common elements of their successes. Did educators at these schools believe they were successful because of a particular program or scripted curriculum? They did not. Did they attribute their successes to supportive parents or unusually cooperative children? No. Each of these schools had good curriculum and qualified teachers. Some had supportive parents. They had staff development and many other components that most elementary schools share. But they had something else.

Significant practices set these elementary schools apart from less successful schools. These practices are simple to understand but difficult to implement. Every one of these schools developed six exceptional systems, beginning with a culture of universal achievement.

Creating a culture of universal achievement and the other exceptional systems was at the core of every success story. The challenge of educating disadvantaged children is not exceptionally complex. Knowing how to organize a school that creates exceptionally successful students is relatively simple. But doing the work is difficult. It requires teachers and a principal who are tenacious and courageous, who never waver in their commitment to disenfranchised children, and who refuse to give up when they experience inevitable, frustrating bumps in the road.

CHAPTER
2

Developing Exceptional Systems

*Focus 90% of your time on solutions
and only 10% of your time on problems.*

Anthony J. D'Angelo

We began our quest for answers by searching the literature and studying dozens of successful, low-income schools across the nation. We believed if we found unique practices that were common to these elementary schools, we would be able to replicate their successes. We were not disappointed. However, we did not find what we expected. We were looking for silver bullets. We were looking for programs, systems, or software applications we could purchase or adopt that would tip the scales and significantly increase the odds of disadvantaged children being academically successful. We were looking for external, easy fixes, and they just didn't exist. Then we read about the work of Jerry Sternin, and we understood why.

THE PIONEERING WORK OF JERRY STERNIN

Jerry Sternin, director of the Positive Deviance Initiative and former country director for Save the Children, tells of a fascinating experience he had in 1990. While working in the Philippines, he received a request from the government of Vietnam to bring a team of researchers to their country to develop strategies for reducing childhood malnutrition. The government gave Sternin and his team only six months to do this work.

At that time, between sixty and seventy percent of Vietnamese children who lived in villages suffered from some degree of malnutrition. When international organizations provided food, the situation improved. When food deliveries stopped, the problem became worse. It was a vicious cycle, and Vietnamese government officials desperately wanted to find more stable solutions.

Think about why food deliveries from around the world failed to provide these villagers a long-term solution to childhood malnutrition. First, the villagers who received food were passive. They weren't required to change their behaviors. As long as food was delivered, they ate. When deliveries stopped, they starved. Second, food that arrived without even having been requested, like manna falling from the heavens, discouraged efforts by the villagers to seek long-term, systemic solutions to the problems of intermittent malnutrition. These villagers were completely and passively dependent on the outside world, and they had little motivation to change.

When Sternin arrived in Vietnam, he set up operations and began the study of the nutritional status of children in four villages. Immediately he confirmed that many children in these villages suffered from malnutrition. He knew that if his team was to be successful, they needed to identify solutions to this problem that could be sustained locally. It was a huge challenge. As they began their research, Sternin's volunteers asked villagers one simple question: "Are there any well-nourished children in your village who come from unusually poor families? "To their astonishment, the answer was yes. Realizing that in these villages it was possible for poor children to be reasonably nourished proved to be the researchers' aha! moment.

The team identified six families and spent two days with each in an attempt to identify what they did differently, and they discovered something important. Each family did the same three things that were not common in other families throughout their villages. These poor yet reasonably nourished families gathered small shrimp and crabs from the rice paddies and put them on their food; they ate the greens from sweet potato tops; and they fed their children small amounts of food five or six times a day, as opposed to feeding them larger amounts of food twice every day. (When children were fed twice daily, they tended to consume less food over the course of a day because their stomachs were too small to hold enough food in only two sittings.) Because of these three unique practices, children in these six families consumed nearly twice the number of calories as did the other children in their villages. As families in these four villages began to adopt these three simple practices, the curse of childhood malnutrition began to diminish.

Sternin realized that these six families had stumbled upon specific practices that had the potential to positively impact the problem of childhood malnutrition. It is unlikely, however, that he realized how his work with malnourished children in Vietnam would eventually inspire the transformation of elementary schools across America.

Think about the three-step process Jerry Sternin and his team stumbled upon. First, they asked villagers if there were any children in local families who were not struggling from malnutrition. Second, when the answer was yes, Sternin identified exactly what those families did differently. And third, he shared those unique practices with the broader community and encouraged them to do the same.

THE TURNAROUND SCHOOLS MODEL FOR CREATING EXCEPTIONAL SYSTEMS

Los Peñasquitos Elementary School and each of the other high-performing, high-poverty schools we studied inadvertently followed Sternin's three-step process when they created their own successful, break-the-mold exceptional systems. This coincidence was almost too incredible to believe, and it only confirmed the universal importance of this process. After realizing how effectively these schools had used Sternin's three-step process, we modified it and created the following TurnAround Schools model for creating exceptional systems.

1. Identify an individual or a team in your school, or in a school that looks like yours, that succeeds in extraordinary and unexpected ways.

2. Identify the practices that account for their success.

3. Using your own unique resources, replicate the core principles of those practices and turn them into your own exceptional systems.

It's really just that simple. If a silver bullet for the academic success of underrepresented children is to be found, this is it. Think for a moment about why it is so important for teachers and their principal to find their own solutions to the challenges of educating their most needy students rather than relying upon the purported wisdom of others.

First, it's natural for people to resist solutions that come from the outside. We've all heard often-justified cynicism from teachers and administrators when external solutions from above or outside are forced on them. "What do those people know? Have they ever worked with our kids? Who are they to think they know what will work for us?" The tendency for educators to resist outside ideas is just as real as the tendency of a body's immune system to resist foreign substances. It's automatic, and it's usually successful.

Second, even if outside solutions that are imposed on a school are eventually adopted, they are rarely embraced with enthusiasm. This is human nature. Teachers embrace what they create. They often merely tolerate what they are forced to accept.

Third, teachers and principals can find answers to the specific challenges of educating their disadvantaged students. Educators are smart people, and when they believe in their abilities, focus on specific problems, and creatively marshal their resources, they usually find answers that make sense for their school and their students — answers that are willingly embraced by their colleagues.

Learning that the high-achieving, high-poverty schools we studied looked inside to find solutions for achievement challenges was revolutionary! Educators at these successful schools had adopted a very practical attitude — they never expected someone else to hand them pre-packaged answers for educating their most challenging students. They knew that success only comes from an entire staff working together and using their own resources to develop unique, effective practices. These educators had the results to prove it.

THE SIX CORE EXCEPTIONAL SYSTEMS

Several years ago when we began our work, we identified remarkable elementary schools by asking this simple question: Was this a low-income elementary school whose students performed significantly better than what would have been predicted when considering their zip code and demographics? If the answer was yes, we closely examined their practices.

Although we approached this work with an open mind, we were nonetheless surprised to find that each of these schools shared six well-developed exceptional systems. The systems were like a common thread that wove their way through every one of these success stories. The importance placed on these exceptional systems by the educators in these schools was so universal that we were eventually forced to conclude that the practices defined by these systems were largely responsible for the extraordinary success of their students. Each of these schools developed and implemented the following six core exceptional systems:

1. A schoolwide culture of universal achievement
2. Teacher collaboration
3. Classroom lessons aligned to academic standards
4. Classroom assessments that guide instruction and interventions
5. A system for easily managing data
6. Data-driven interventions, both academic and social

It seemed too simple to be true. What school hasn't made at least some attempt to acknowledge the importance of each of these practices? But we couldn't deny what we found. If it is true that these six core exceptional systems define the practices that most predictably result in unexpectedly inspiring student achievement, then schools across America should begin creating their own versions of these exceptional systems today. The children whose futures depend on what these schools do don't have an extra year, or even a week, to wait.

THE PROCESS

Great principals dream big. While most people must see before they believe, great principals have the ability to believe before they see. That is why they can inspire teachers to step into the dark with only a promise that successful students await them on the other side.

Great principals also know how to organize others around visions of excellence. They understand that their job is to lead the process of creating exceptional systems. They know that if a project is to be embraced by teachers, teachers must also be convinced that the exceptional system is essential to the success of their students. Everyone must assume ownership of this project.

Before the work of developing any exceptional system begins, realistic principals will have casual, off-line conversations with several teacher-leaders about the system they are considering. Principals will learn a lot from these discussions.

They will get a sense for how the idea will be embraced by other teachers, and they'll also hear concerns that need to be anticipated. Floating these trial balloons before any formal work begins is essential to the success of a project. When teacher-leaders agree that the work is important, the principal will have gained influential allies.

LEADERSHIP COMMITTEE

The next step is to convene a leadership committee that ideally includes the principal, one respected representative from each grade level, and other key leaders. This committee does most of the work and communicates back and forth between their group and grade-level teams.

When developing an exceptional system, the role of the Leadership Committee has three tasks:

1. Define the problem.

2. Identify examples of success that already exist on campus or at high-performing schools with similar student demographics.

3. Lead the collaborative process that allows everyone to participate in the development of a unique system based upon these models of success.

For example, suppose that the system being considered is teacher collaboration. The first job of the leadership committee in this situation is to define the problem. How do teachers currently collaborate? How is their current practice less than satisfactory?

The second step is to find one or more teams on campus that collaborate in ways that contribute directly to the academic achievement of every student and then identify the specific practices that make their collaboration so effective. If no examples of excellence can be found on campus, the Leadership Team must lead the search for innovative and successful practices at other schools.

The third step is for the Leadership Team to work with teachers as they grapple with these issues, eventually creating a written draft document that represents the staff's unique solution to the challenge of collaboration.

Back and Forth

Open communication throughout this process is essential. All teachers must feel they are a part of the process. From the beginning of the process to the end, conversations go back and forth between the leadership team and grade-level teams. Following each meeting, committee representatives make full reports to their team members and then record the input they are given. The principal also meets formally and informally with grade-level teams and individuals. Principal outreach at this stage is essential because she can answer questions, reinforce core values, and help generate consensus.

What will evolve during this process is a draft document that clearly identifies why the staff collaborates, when they will collaborate, what the focus of that collaboration will be, and the group norms that will help maintain the integrity of the collaborative process into the future.

Reaching Substantial Consensus

The next step is delicate and critical. The entire staff is brought together to formally consider the draft document. Many principals feel this meeting should be co-facilitated by teacher representatives. At the meeting, each teacher has an opportunity to ask questions and provide input. The goal is to reach substantial consensus when an overwhelming majority of the group agrees to move forward. Striving for absolute consensus is not always practical. One or two staff members who refuse to work for the benefit of all children should never be allowed to derail the efforts of the majority.

The staff may reach substantial consensus quickly, or some negotiation may still need to take place. Either way, it will be a great day for the school when substantial consensus is reached. It will be an even greater day for the teachers because they will have worked together to formally create their first core exceptional system.

THE ENDORSEMENT

There remains one more step that can never be neglected. This last step requires heart and commitment. Without it, the newly created exceptional system may find its way into a dusty file cabinet, never to be seen again. The last step is for the entire staff to endorse the exceptional system with their own signatures.

An endorsement is a statement signed by all staff members, signifying that they will abide by the contents of the document that describes the exceptional system. This can be easily done by preparing a one-page sheet with everyone's typed name and a short statement at the top. For example, "The Undersigned Support Central Elementary School's Collaboration Commitment." The signed endorsement is put in a frame and proudly hung on the office wall next to the collaboration commitment. What a powerful statement this makes! A copy of the Los Peñasquitos Collaboration Commitment can be found in Appendix A.

We are always asked, "What do you do if a teacher refuses to sign the endorsement?" The answer is simple: Just hang the endorsement without the teacher's signature. You obviously need a substantial consensus, but if you have a resister (or two), never wait to move forward until they finally agree. You could wait forever, and your students don't have that long. The worst that can happen is that your superintendent, a reporter, or a parent will come into your office, read the commitment and see the signatures, and then ask, "Why didn't Mr. Jones sign the endorsement?" If that were to happen to us, we'd just say, "We really don't know. He's down in Room 8. Why don't you walk down to his classroom and ask him?" In the meantime, the rest of your staff will be collaborating together and experiencing very impressive results.

Exceptional or Not?

So what makes a system exceptional?

- The entire staff is involved in its creation.

- It draws upon resources that currently exist in the school.

- A written document defines why the system is important, what will be done, when it will happen, and how teachers will be involved.

- Teachers formally endorse their work.

Without these features, a system is not exceptional, and without exceptional systems a school cannot be exceptional. This is sometimes hard for people to understand.

Jeff spoke with the superintendent of a one-school district not long ago. This superintendent's school is in Year Three of Program Improvement. A large percentage of the children at his school are second language learners who live in generational poverty. As hard as the teachers work, their results continued to be very disappointing. "Superintendent Smith" and several of his teachers had just attended one of our institutes where they learned about the relationship between the six core exceptional systems and exceptional academic results. He was almost giddy as he spoke. "We were just thrilled to realize we are already doing all those things!" It was all Jeff could do to keep his mouth shut and not ask the question that seemed so obvious: "If you're already doing the right things, why aren't more of your students learning?"

This conversation with Dr. Smith highlighted some very important points. His teachers do collaborate. They made some efforts to align their curriculum to the academic standards. They administer some assessments. So what didn't Dr. Smith understand? He didn't understand that their practices were stale. He didn't understand that his teachers were in a rut, doing what they always did and not

really knowing why. He didn't understand that mu
took place at the school was primarily designed t(
needs of adults. He didn't understand that the
place at his school were not exceptional. If systems aɪc ɪɪυι
exceptional, neither is a school.

Remember this simple rule: exceptional schools have
exceptional systems — always.

MAKING YOUR SCHOOL EXCEPTIONAL

We wrote the next chapters with elementary educators in
mind. We wrote them for you. We walk in your shoes, we
know your challenges, and we appreciate the work you do
with your students. We also know that you don't have time
to sort through abstract, often controversial arguments that
provide endless opportunities for scholarly debate. You want
practical, reasonable, tested solutions that get results and
that you can begin implementing tomorrow. You will not be
disappointed.

The next chapters describe each of the six exceptional
systems in detail. We present the exceptional systems in the
order we do because the systems are like a staircase. Each
one naturally leads to the next, and they should be created
in the following order:

- A schoolwide culture of universal achievement

- Teacher collaboration

- Classroom lessons aligned to academic standards

- Classroom assessments that guide instruction and
  interventions

- A system for easily managing data

- Data-driven interventions, both academic and social

A Schoolwide Culture
of Universal Achievement

First, teachers and administrators must join together in believing that disadvantaged children can be successful and that the collective efforts of the school will be sufficient to make that dream a reality. Once this belief is in place, energy that was previously expended by arguing and making excuses will go directly into neutralizing many of the challenges students bring to school.

Teacher Collaboration

After work has begun at a school to create a culture of universal achievement, the next exceptional system that needs to be created describes how teachers will collaborate effectively. The development of every other system requires collaborative efforts, so developing this system makes the creation of future exceptional systems possible. Focus on creating an exceptional system for collaboration, do it right, commit it to writing, and you'll be on your way to greatness.

CLASSROOM LESSONS
ALIGNED TO ACADEMIC STANDARDS

Once teachers collaborate effectively, they can use those skills to design common grade-level lessons that reflect academic standards. This is difficult work, and it is only made possible by teachers who know how to work well together.

CLASSROOM ASSESSMENTS THAT GUIDE
INSTRUCTION AND INTERVENTIONS

After lessons are created that target academic standards, teachers need a way to gauge if their lessons were effective, identify which students are not on track for becoming proficient, and determine exactly what areas of learning need additional attention. Creating or acquiring the right classroom assessments and developing a plan for their administration are at the heart of this system.

A SYSTEM FOR EASILY
MANAGING DATA

Assessments inevitably generate data. If this data is to be available and useful to teachers, a simple system must be in place to manage it well.

DATA-DRIVEN INTERVENTIONS,
BOTH ACADEMIC AND SOCIAL

Once student achievement data is easily available, that data will be used to identify students who are not on track for becoming proficient in the core academic areas. When teachers use data to identify individual students who are not on track and what specific areas they need remediation, then teachers can customize interventions to meet the specific needs of each child.

These six systems are not new to most schools, but making them exceptional leads to extraordinary academic achievement for disadvantaged children. As we stated previously, forget about finding a silver bullet. The answer to closing the achievement gap is creating these systems, making them exceptional and unique, and ensuring that they are central to the work of your school. Do this and your students will be well on their way to college.

Chapter Summary

Developing Exceptional Systems

Key Points

- The key strategy for closing the achievement gap is creating the six core systems, making them exceptional and unique, and ensuring that they are central to the work of your school.

- While working in the jungles of Vietnam, Jerry Sternin discovered that the most effective way to reduce childhood malnutrition in villages was to find local examples of poor families whose children were not malnourished, find out what they did differently, and then encourage other villagers to do the same. This model also works brilliantly for schools that seek to find answers to student achievement challenges that seemingly have no solutions.

- We call this the TurnAround Schools Model for Creating Exceptional Systems. It has three steps:

   a. Identify an individual or a team in your school, or in a school that looks like yours, that succeeds in extraordinary and unexpected ways.

   b. Identify the practices that account for their success.

   c. Using your own unique resources, replicate the core principles of those practices and turn them into your own exceptional systems.

- Six core exceptional systems define the work of teachers in every high-achieving, high-poverty school. These systems are:

  a. A schoolwide culture of universal achievement

  b. Teacher collaboration

  c. Classroom lessons aligned to academic standards

  d. Classroom assessments that guide instruction and interventions

  e. A system for easily managing data

  f. Data driven interventions, both academic and social

- If schools want their students to beat the academic odds, they will carefully and deliberately develop unique versions of these six exceptional systems, and they will do so by using TurnAround Schools Model for Creating Exceptional Systems.

- Maverick principals thoughtfully lead their teachers in the collaborative process of creating exceptional systems.

CHAPTER

3

Creating a Schoolwide Culture of Universal Achievement

"Some things have to be believed to be seen."

Ralph Hodgson

Exceptional elementary schools do not spring into existence by accident. People do not wake up one day to discover that doing what they always did finally results in academic excellence. That's not how it works. Creating learning revolutions at formerly struggling elementary schools takes strategic planning. It requires short-term planning that directs the staff's focus on a weekly basis, and it requires long-term planning that guides the practices and encourages the heart from one year to the next. With this strategic planning, a school will eventually become a model for fostering academic excellence for all children. It's inevitable.

The first and most important task for elementary reform is to create a culture of universal achievement. Before that happens, a school may still experience slow, halting improvements that are compelled by local or federal mandates. These small successes will likely be celebrated, or at least acknowledged, but an undercurrent of cynicism and discontent will

27

remain because certain staff members (often those who are most vocal) will continue to argue that it is unreasonable, even impossible, to expect that every student is capable of academic proficiency. The "soft bigotry of low expectations" will continue to be an anchor pulling against the tide of possibilities. It is impossible for a school to become a solid academic powerhouse if it doesn't first embrace a culture of universal achievement.

Exactly what do we mean by a schoolwide culture of universal achievement? At a school where this culture is embraced, everyone believes that every student is capable of academic proficiency and that the primary responsibility for making that success a reality rests with the adults. This belief is crucial to creating an exceptional school. Of course, it should be understood that we are excluding from this sweeping commitment any child who suffers from serious cognitive challenges.

Believing that every student is capable of academic success is not enough. That belief, if it stands alone, puts responsibility for learning squarely on the shoulders of students. It's less common to hear this anymore, but many of us still remember teachers smugly proclaiming, "I teach 'em. If they choose to learn, that's their business."

Agreeing that all children *can* be successful is easy because doing so requires no personal accountability on the part of teachers or administrators. But admitting that the school can have a far greater influence on the academic achievement of disadvantaged students than do families or neighborhoods or cultures is something very different.

It's not difficult to understand why teachers and principals often resist agreeing with that arguably radical concept. When adults take primary responsibility for student learning, they must accept personal accountability for student performance even when they can't control the social challenges students bring into the classroom. Taking this leap of faith can be frightening because it is fundamentally unfair to ask people to be accountable for anything they can't control.

But the good news is that schools can influence and neutralize (not eliminate) many of the challenges children bring with them into the classroom. To understand and accept this premise can fundamentally change the professional lives of teachers and principals. If this statement is true (it is), and if educators can learn how to influence and neutralize these challenges (they can), then they can seize control of student learning in ways that were previously never imagined. This is actually happening every day at exceptional elementary schools across the nation, and poor, minority, first generation, and disadvantaged students are learning. It can also happen at your school.

WHAT DOES A CULTURE OF UNIVERSAL ACHIEVEMENT LOOK LIKE?

Every school with a staff that embraces a culture of universal achievement will share common beliefs and commitments, and these will be deeply embedded into their daily conversations and practices. You will seldom hear or see anything that violates these core beliefs or dishonors the hopeful efforts of the staff as they work tirelessly to create a school where every student is academically successful.

We have identified six beliefs shared by schools that embrace a culture of universal achievement. Ponder these beliefs. Ask yourself to what degree everyone on your staff shares them. Think about strategies you can help to introduce that will weave these beliefs even more tightly into the fabric of your school.

BELIEF 1: EVERY STUDENT WILL BE PROFICIENT IN READING, WRITING, AND MATHEMATICS

Children learn many things in school. They learn to read and write and do math. They learn about social studies, art, music, and physical education. They also learn to share and be respectful. Good schools truly address the social and curricular needs of the whole child.

tend, however, that three academic subjects are non-negotiables and that every student must be proficient in each of these subjects by the time they leave elementary school. These three academic non-negotiables are fundamental to the future academic success of every student, and they can never be compromised. If students don't master these by the time they leave elementary school, they will never compete successfully with more affluent students in middle and high school. The three academic non-negotiables are reading, writing, and mathematics.

At the school where we worked as principals, students attend class for one hundred eighty days each year. After factoring out recess and lunch, children are actually in the classroom for about five hours each day. That means in an entire year, children and teacher are only together for nine hundred hours. Few people would agree that nine hundred hours is enough time to make sure every student masters every curricular expectation. But nine hundred hours is a fact of life in almost every classroom in America.

Because there are only so many minutes in the day, everything can't be taught. This reality obligates teachers to make difficult decisions: "This group of six children needs an extra thirty minutes of reading instruction, but I also have an art lesson to teach." Or, "I've only scheduled two hours this week to teach writing, but now my grade-level team wants to add a PE rotation." Limited time and extraordinary student needs force teachers to face these difficult decisions, and our best teachers know that when their backs are against the wall and they have to choose, they never sacrifice reading, writing or mathematics — ever.

Why is that? Students who enter middle school unable to write clearly and persuasively, read with understanding, and attack mathematics with confidence are quickly sorted out and subtly (or not so subtly) identified as not being on a college track. The system labels these students as not being college bound, and the children hear that message loud and clear. For the purpose of this sorting, it doesn't matter if kids are good at art. Nobody cares if they can name all the state capitals. But not being competent in reading, writing or math is the kiss of death. The sad truth is that in middle school many of these struggling children soon become frustrated and drift toward academic mediocrity, losing whatever desire they once had to attend college and embrace the American dream. For these children, the battle is lost.

The stakes are just too high for underrepresented students. If the critical deadline is the transition from elementary to middle school, and if proficiency in reading, writing and mathematics holds the key to academic success, then it should come as no surprise that the first belief at every school that embraces a culture of universal achievement is that every student, without exception and without excuse, will be proficient in reading, writing, and mathematics.

BELIEF 2: THE ACADEMIC ACCOMPLISHMENT OF EVERY STUDENT IS AN OBSESSION

It is common for many students in low-income elementary schools to be behind grade level in the core academic areas for reasons that are understandable and legitimate. But middle school approaches whether students are ready or not. The clock is ticking.

One parent who understood this urgency was Lacretia Jones. She and her daughter LaTonia lived across the street from Los Peñasquitos in federally subsidized housing. One afternoon in the spring of 2007, Ms. Jones saw Jeff from a distance and with a stern voice, hollered for him to come over. She was not a mother to be trifled with, and Jeff promptly responded.

"Mr. King," she began, "I'm sick and tired of walking my daughter every morning from my apartment to this school, and then walking her back to that apartment again every afternoon!"   This took him by surprise."I don't understand, Ms. Jones. I've been to your apartment, and it's not that far."

...at's right, you don't understand. I'm sick and tired of walking my LaTonia from *that* apartment in the morning and returning to *that* apartment in the afternoon. When my daughter grows up, I want her to put her children in a car and drive them to school, just like your wife did when your children were young. And in the afternoon, I want my daughter to pick her up children and drive them back to their home — a real house — just like your wife did every afternoon. That's what I want for LaTonia." Then she continued. "And I want to thank you and LaTonia's teachers for believing in her and for helping to make that dream a possibility. I can't do it on my own, but you're helping me. Next year when she goes to middle school, we're really going to miss Los Peñasquitos. But LaTonia's catching up. She's real proud of herself and wants to go to college. Thank you, Mr. King."

We all have LaTonias and Ms. Joneses in our schools. We have significant obligations to these parents and children, and the stakes are huge. If we fail, their children will fail. The odds are against us, and we only have a few short years to create learning miracles. Understanding this, educators, especially at exceptional low-income elementary schools, always have an intense, impatient obsession about the academic achievement of every student.

BELIEF 3: THE SCHOOL CAN NEUTRALIZE MANY CHALLENGES CHILDREN BRING TO THE CLASSROOM

One evening on a flight from San Francisco, Jeff struck up a conversation with a sixth grade teacher who happened to be seated next to him. When Jeff said he was an elementary school principal, the floodgates opened. Jeff heard about crappy parents, kids who were out of control, and administrators who had forgotten what it was like to be a teacher. He heard about gangs, neglect, and laziness. He got an earful about No Child Left Behind. This teacher was a man who felt powerless to impact his students and who hated his job. It was obvious that he really didn't even like many of his students.

Jeff was saddened, offended, and defensive. But in an attempt to be civil, he told the teacher about his Title 1 school where the kids spoke thirty-five languages and lived in a huge welfare complex across the street. Jeff described how happy the teaching staff was, how well the students performed, how almost every one of them was working hard to go to college, and how the staff figured out ways to neutralize many of the challenges the kids bring into the classrooms. Jeff told him that we promise our parents that their children will be able to read and write and do math at grade level.

The teacher stared at Jeff, shook his head, and said, "Do you know what kind of legal predicament that would cause for me? I could get sued." It was all Jeff could do to keep from laughing. Or crying.

Jeff has replayed that conversation over and over again in his head. At one time this sixth grade teacher was probably bright-eyed and hopeful. What had happened over the years? What turned an energetic new teacher into a broken, miserable excuse for an educator? Perhaps he gradually began to believe that he was powerless as an individual to overcome the negative impacts that poverty inflicts on his students, and eventually he just gave up.

What would have made a difference for this teacher? Is it possible for a school to compensate for many of the challenges kids bring to the classroom? What about kids who show up to school hungry? Students whose parents won't come to Back to School Night? Latch key children who roam the streets into the night? Children who won't do their homework and whose parents couldn't care less? Kids who come from good families but only hear another language at home? Children who have a parent in jail or in a gang?

Educators whose students face challenges like these have a choice to make. Either we can step up and neutralize (not solve) many of these challenges, or we can accept defeat like the teacher on the plane. There is no middle ground. For every challenge we neutralize, we gain power to influence the

...emic future of students. For every challenge we refuse to confront, we diminish our own potential as educators.

This is messy work, but it is doable. Let's pick off a few of the challenges listed above.

If kids arrive to school hungry, don't waste your time trying to convince their parents to feed them a nutritious breakfast. Instead, work with your food services department to provide meals for these students before school starts. Many districts do this, and the Free and Reduced Lunch Program covers the costs. If that doesn't work, find something that does. Perhaps a church will make peanut butter sandwiches for the kids or a local grocery store will provide fruit. Maybe some obscure budget account can be used to buy granola bars. There's always an answer, but the answer may not be one that is obvious. When kids have full stomachs, they are ready to learn.

If children arrive to school feeling neglected and unloved, don't complain about how impossible that makes your job. Turn your school into an emotional sanctuary. Provide the unconditional love and guidance that parents should rightfully be giving their children at home. Make the hours your children spend at school feel like living with the most supportive family a child could imagine. Love these children. Set the bar high. Believe in their potential. Support them. Discipline them. Do all this unconditionally. As they walk into your school in the morning, children will feel as though they are walking from darkness into light. Smiles will appear, they will relax, and they will trust. The hours they spend in your classrooms will have a far greater influence on their lives than the hours they spend outside of school. When kids feel loved and emotionally secure, they are ready to learn.

If some of your students are latch key kids, roaming the neighborhood unsupervised into the evening, don't lament the fact that irresponsible parents make learning impossible. Do something about it. When Los Peñasquitos Elementary School faced this exact challenge ten years ago, there were no obvious solutions to the problem. Jeff eventually requested a meeting with the pastor of the local church. This pastor had expressed a tentative interest in working with Los Peñasquitos' students in some capacity. After some short negotiations and with an understanding about the limits of their involvement, they struck a deal where the church provided the people, the money, and the program, and the school provided the space and kids. It was a match made in heaven. Ten years later, that partnership is still going strong. Over one hundred twenty children are currently in the program. Can you imagine such a thing? One hundred twenty students every day are now cared for before and after school by some of the kindest people you could ever hope to meet. Church volunteers serve breakfast in the morning and snacks in the afternoon, and after school they tutor children, organize sports activities, and teach lessons from the Character Counts℠ program. When caring adults supervise kids and provide them with opportunities that support the goals of the school, children are ready to learn.

For another inspiring story of practical solutions, consider Geoffrey Canada, a modern day hero. As a child, he experienced life in Central Harlem. He knew that without significant intervention, children in that community had very little chance to break free of the bonds of generational poverty. Canada decided that he needed to neutralize the challenges these children faced, and he refused to wait for someone else to do it. 1n 1997, he established the Harlem Children's Zone for the express purpose of proving that poor black children can and will achieve. He adopted one hundred square blocks in Central Harlem and set about to meet the needs of all eight thousand children who lived in that area. This is a man who lives and breathes a culture of universal achievement. He dreamed big because big dreams were the only things that could make a difference in those one hundred square blocks.

Geoffrey Canada rolled up his sleeves and went to work. He organized the Baby College that offers free parenting classes to new parents living in the Harlem Children's Zone. He started the Promise Academy Charter Schools so children in the Zone can take advantage of a quality education. At these schools, he set up free health clinics and offers free gourmet meals served in a restaurant style setting. His students study Suzuki violin, learn to play chess, and practice martial arts. Hundreds of children from Central Harlem are now in college because of the dreams and dedication of this one man.

Few people will ever accomplish a modern day learning miracle that rivals the Harlem Children's Zone. But if Geoffrey Canada can successfully take on the challenges of one hundred square blocks in one of America's toughest neighborhoods, can you also successfully address many of the learning challenges faced by disadvantaged children in your school? We challenge you to be inspired by Geoffrey Canada and create learning miracles for the underrepresented students in your small corner of the world.

The point of this section should be clear. There are no silver bullets for managing the challenges children bring to school. You cannot expect to find success by buying a book or hiring a consultant who will tell you exactly what to do. But when teachers and a principal muster extraordinary courage, step far outside the status-quo box, and roll up their sleeves and get to work, they can find answers where answers never before existed.

Belief 4: Student Achievement Is the Number One Topic of Conversation

There is an old saying that if you want to change the culture, you must first change the conversation. Lots of things get talked about at schools, but what dominates those conversations? That of course depends on the school. It could be curriculum. It might be the demands of No Child Left Behind. Perhaps conversations revolve around an unpopular principal or a perception by teachers that they aren't being properly supported. Or maybe the most common conversation is about academic results. In too many schools, it isn't.

One feature that stands out at exceptional turnaround elementary schools is that teachers and principals are impassioned by the challenge of student achievement, and student achievement at these schools is the focus of most conversations. We believe there is a direct correlation between those passionate conversations and the academic success of students. If this relationship truly exists, the challenge for teachers and principals becomes how to encourage these focused conversations at their school.

Doing so really isn't difficult. One advantage a principal or teacher leader has is access to the bully pulpit. They can stand before people, speak, and people have to listen. Leaders can set agendas and influence priorities. They can guide conversations. They can establish deadlines. They can greatly influence the development of a vision. Each of these actions will change conversations that take place on campus. Making student achievement the number one conversation at a school is within the grasp of every principal and teacher leader.

BELIEF 5: A MAVERICK SPIRIT IS LEADING THE WAY

Do you know educational leaders who are so exceptional, so effective, and so superb that you stand in awe at their abilities? Have you heard stories of others? Many of us have seen the movie Stand and Deliver that tells the story of Jaime Escalante and his Hispanic scholars at Garfield High School. Geoffrey Canada and his extraordinary Children's Learning Zone were highlighted earlier in this chapter. Others have heard the equally impressive stories of Michael Feinberg, who co-founded the KIPP Academy, or Nancy Ichinaga, the legendary former principal of Bennett-Kew Elementary School in Inglewood, California. What stands out about these individuals? What makes them so extraordinary? They are all maverick leaders.

Maverick leaders are never afraid to stand before a group of teachers or the community and boldly declare that every student will be academically proficient in the core academic areas and that the primary responsibility of the school is to make that happen. They are like a jukebox that only plays one song. Whenever they speak, they have only one message, a message of hope and high expectations that inspires those they lead to create miracles.

To outside observers, maverick leaders are fearless. They refuse to be boxed in by status-quo thinking. They look at disadvantaged children and only see potential. Maverick leaders fight the system when that system is sluggish or ambivalent about getting results. Nothing sets off a maverick leader more quickly than being told that disadvantaged kids can't learn or that the school has to "go slow to go fast." Going slow to go fast is too often an excuse to go slow to do nothing at all. These leaders look into the eyes of each child whose life depends on what happens that day in school, and they know there is no time to waste.

Maverick leaders carefully and deliberately foster respectful, trusting, and collaborative relationships with their teachers and colleagues. Developing these relationships may possibly be the most important task maverick leaders do. They never forget that the rubber meets the road in those thousands of daily interactions between teachers and students, and maverick leaders do everything possible to clear away roadblocks that may get in the way of those interactions.

Maverick leaders think big and organize people around those big ideas. They don't waste time getting started. Because teachers respect maverick principals, teachers are usually willing to follow their leadership and work collaboratively with them to find innovative and bold solutions.

Are maverick leaders born or made? Who knows? We suspect it's a little of both. But the truth is that no school can become truly great unless a maverick leader is at the helm. Your job is to either use your maverick leadership skills to encourage greatness or to do whatever it takes to become that maverick leader.

Belief 6: There Are No Excuses for Poor Effort

Many of our students have broken spirits at the beginning of the school year, and we do what all caring educators do — we create a safe and secure world for them. We are there with loving arms and listening ears, and that's more than many of our students can expect from their parents.

Unfortunately, some of our colleagues with the biggest hearts also have a very difficult time holding these students accountable for academic excellence, and their reasons are obvious. After all, how could a caring teacher demand that a child rise above her heartache and struggle to master difficult academic content after the child just saw her mother driven off to jail (or saw her cousin beaten by a drunk dad, or was yelled at just before leaving home, or you-fill-in-the-blank)? These well-intentioned teachers forget that if their students ever hope to escape the grasp of generational poverty, they will do so only if they are very well educated. And to eventually be well educated, elementary students must be proficient in the core academic areas.

Of course we are compassionate when our students' lives swirl in chaos, but the greatest gift we can give them is to never accept excuses for poor effort, even when these students are in pain. This is tough to accept and even more difficult to put into practice. But it is absolutely necessary.

As an example, consider DeQuan. In the fall of 2006, he and his sister landed at Los Peñasquitos Elementary School with quite a story:

One cold fall night in New York a fire broke out in their small rented house. DeQuan, his younger sister, and their mother escaped. Their father died in the flames. Having no reason to stay in New York, DeQuan's mother pulled together the few dollars she had, put her children into their old car, and headed for San Diego where a friend lived in the federally subsidized complex across from Los Peñasquitos Elementary. As they approached Las Vegas, their car died. DeQuan's mother took their few remaining dollars and bought bus tickets to San Diego.

We still remember that rainy day in early November when DeQuan's mother enrolled her two children in school. We heard her story and felt genuine compassion for these two children. We placed them with wonderful, caring teachers, and we offered them every service that was available.

Later that school year, DeQuan's teacher came to Damen's office and told him that DeQuan was working far below his ability. She said DeQuan appeared to be sad, and for very good reasons. "Would you talk with him?" she asked.

Shortly afterward DeQuan appeared at Damen's office. Damen invited him to sit down and talk about what was going on. DeQuan knew why he was sent, and he told Mr. Lopez that he was sad because his father had died and because he missed his friends. They talked for a few minutes about these tragedies and how the school was helping his sister and him cope.

Then Damen asked DeQuan if he liked living in the apartment with the other family.

"No, I hate it. I sleep on the couch. I don't even have my own room."

He then asked if DeQuan wanted to live like that forever.

"No way, Mr. Lopez. I want to live in a house and have a nice car and a job."

"Well then, DeQuan, let me ask you something else. Do you think you're the only student at this school who has problems? Let me tell you — you're not. There are lots of kids here who have problems, and some of those problems are worse than yours. You're not alone. And you know what I tell those other kids? I tell them that if they ever hope to live in a nice house and drive a nice car and have a good job, they have to work hard in school even though they have problems. And I'm telling you the same thing."

"Now, we're going to stand up, go back to your classroom, and you're going to walk in, sit down, and get to work. And when I stop by this afternoon, I expect to see you working. And tomorrow, I'm going to sneak in when you don't expect me, and I better see you working. Are you okay with that?"

DeQuan was taken aback, but he agreed, and he went back to work.

There's a happy ending to this story. That first year, DeQuan's test scores were average in math and below average in reading and writing. We were not surprised. But the following year, his test scores were high average in all three areas. At least in DeQuan's case, holding him accountable to very high expectations and accepting no excuses for poor effort paid off. His future is bright, and if we were betting men, we would give odds that someday he will end up with that nice house, the new car, and a good job that he loves.

Creating a Schoolwide Culture of Universal Achievement

KEY POINTS

- The overriding belief at a school that embraces a culture of universal achievement is that every student is capable of academic proficiency, and that the primary responsibility for making that proficiency a reality rests with the adults.

- No responsible educator can say that it is impossible for high-poverty children to be high-achieving students because it is happening today in schools across America. The only question is, quite simply, does a principal and her teachers have the passion and determination to make same dream a reality at their school?

- A courageous principal and equally courageous teacher-leaders encourage the creation of a culture of universal achievement by focusing relentlessly on student academic achievement and by leading positive conversations with their colleagues.

- A culture of universal achievement is firmly in place when the following beliefs and practices are held by teachers and the principal:

    a. Every student will be proficient in reading, writing and mathematics.

b. The academic accomplishment of every student is an obsession.

c. The school can neutralize many challenges children bring to the classroom.

d. Student achievement is the number one topic of conversation.

e. A maverick spirit is leading the way.

f. There are no excuses for poor effort.

C H A P T E R

4

Teacher Collaboration

*Determine that the thing can and shall be done,
and then we shall find the way.*

Abraham Lincoln

Anne Fox Elementary School in District 54 (Schaumburg, Illinois) is a turnaround school with an inspiring story. In 2005 when Nick Myers was selected as the new principal, students at Anne Fox were struggling. The school had its share of challenges: the children spoke thirty-five languages and twenty eight percent of them received free or reduced-price lunches. The performance of Anne Fox students ranked dead last (and it wasn't even close) among the twenty-one schools in District 54. Ranking last was embarrassing and unacceptable for Nick and his staff, but Nick was a maverick leader who refused to let students' challenges stand in the way of their success.

At the end of his first year as principal, Nick met with his staff, and they had a heart-to-heart conversation about the academic potential of their students. Together, they agreed they would do whatever it took to make the students at Anne Fox the top-achieving students in their district. They also agreed that this crazy goal would be impossible to accomplish unless they took a fresh look at everything they did.

One of the first problems the staff recognized was that formal teacher collaboration was spotty at best. It wasn't that teachers didn't talk — they did. But their master schedule didn't provide opportunities for common planning, and the culture of the school didn't support structured teacher collaboration. When teams did meet it was to discuss matters like field trips or student discipline. Nick said, "These meetings were rarely used to discuss academic achievement, and we certainly weren't looking specifically at the learning needs of every student."

The staff began revamping their master schedule to create frequent opportunities for common planning. They used that newly created time to analyze student data, devise interventions for students who were not yet academically proficient, and help students create individual student goals. As they focused on meeting the academic needs of each individual child, the staff began to see surprising and encouraging results.

In three years, despite the most challenging demographics of any school in the district, Anne Fox's students ranked eleventh in a district of twenty-one elementary schools! As Nick says, "There's no limit to the academic potential of our students. Our system of collaboration is central to ensuring that we maximize their learning potential." Knowing Nick and his very dedicated staff, we suspect their best years are still ahead.

A Sense of Urgency

Having an exceptional system for collaboration is only important if a staff's commitment to underrepresented children is so strong that they are compelled to question status quo thinking and practices and then consider other options that may be unfamiliar and untested. This enthusiasm requires a framework for organizing people, and an exceptional system for collaboration is perfectly suited to that task.

We often hear educators say, "We know our students can achieve so much more, but we just don't know what else to do." The courageous ones go on to say, "There have to be answers out there somewhere. No one else has come up with any bright ideas, so it's up to us. We're the only ones who can figure this out because we're the only ones who know our kids. And we have to begin today, because our students don't have a day to lose." When a staff feels this measure of urgency, they are ready to collaborate.

To tackle these demanding challenges, a Leadership Team must first follow the TurnAround Schools model for creating exceptional systems and define the problem, determine if any examples of extraordinary collaboration currently exist on the campus or at similar schools, and then identify what their successful colleagues are doing to get the results they do. The staff will then collaboratively create and endorse their own unique, formal, written plan for working together that clarifies their commitment and answers the following questions:

- What are the real reasons teachers should meet to focus on the academic achievement of every student?

- When will collaboration take place?

- What exactly will happen in those meetings?

- What common meeting norms will be in place to ensure that meetings are focused and effective?

Creating this formal collaboration plan is the first project a staff must take on once they are ready to break out of status quo thinking and practices. Don't presume that just because teachers meet and talk, their system for collaboration is exceptional. It may be, but most likely it is not. If essential questions have not been answered, if your collaboration commitment is not in writing, or if the vast majority of your teachers have not endorsed it, you still have work to do.

This chapter challenges you to honestly look at your own system for collaboration and decide if it is average or exceptional. If it is average, do what it takes to make it exceptional. Elements commonly found in average and exceptional systems of collaboration are described below. Use these as guidelines when planning your next steps. Never forget that the power of exceptional systems always derives from a group of teachers and their principal flouting conventional wisdom, confronting established practices, and struggling together to create unique solutions to the unique challenges faced by their deserving students. That's when miracles begin.

AVERAGE COLLABORATION

Average collaboration is usually found in schools where the staff is satisfied to do what has always been done. Often, the staff at these schools believe that the job of teachers is to teach, the job of students is to learn, and poor academic achievement is the result of unengaged children and irresponsible parents. Seldom do teachers and administrators at these schools accept that their own beliefs and practices may be the primary cause of poor student achievement. If teachers believe that poor student achievement really is the fault of kids and their parents, they seldom see the need to meet to examine their beliefs and practices.

When Jeff taught math at a middle school in the early years, he fell victim to this same excuse making. When he gave a test and most of his students failed, he told them they were obviously irresponsible and made it clear that he expected them to work harder. He put the blame on his students for their failure to learn because, clearly, he had done his job — he taught them. They just chose to ignore his good teaching. It wasn't until several years later that he realized (or accepted) the fact that when large numbers of his students did not learn concepts, it was because he had done a poor job of teaching. Their lack of success was mostly his responsibility, not theirs. That wasn't easy to admit, but it was the truth. When he moved beyond narrowly teaching the material with a focus an entire class and began to meet the learning needs of individual students, they began to experience the success that he always suspected they were capable of. It wasn't until he examined his beliefs and practices that his students began to reach their academic potential.

This same principle holds true for all teachers. It's not until the staff becomes humble and introspective that they will embrace the need for formal collaboration. At schools where large numbers of children are not meeting academic standards, teachers and their principal must swallow their pride and accept responsibility for those disappointing results. They have to admit that their school must do a better job of neutralizing many of the challenges students bring into their classrooms, and then collaborate together to identify strategies that will allow them to do so. That's not easy to do, but there is no other answer.

TOP DOWN MANDATES

When schools first begin the process of examining their own practices and beliefs, it is usually in response to top-down mandates for change. These mandates typically come directly from the central office but are originally motivated by community, state, or federal demands for improvement. Because of the sense of urgency felt by superintendents and other district administrators, these top-down directives are often accompanied by expedient strategies designed to "fix" schools. When district supervisors say these one-size-fits-all strategies must be implemented, they must be implemented. (In times of crisis, even otherwise prudent administrators may forget that real change in public schools can only percolate from the bottom up and never from the other direction.) Good teachers will rise to the challenge, and average systems of collaboration will spring into existence that allow teachers to respond to these sometimes desperate, top-down, external edicts.

Teachers who find themselves in this situation collaborate primarily for four reasons:

- They feel compelled to do so.

- They must figure out how to implement new instructional decrees.

- Lessons and class activities need to be coordinated, and issues of common interest related to the new strategies must to be discussed.

- Teachers often enjoy each other's company.

To outside observers, this level of forced collaboration creates a façade of competency. It appears that people are effectively working together, and in some respects they are. As a result of these meetings, plans for implementing newly mandated instructional strategies are negotiated. In moments of quiet rebellion, teachers may even courageously bend a rule or two in attempts to make these strategies more palatable to the cultures of their own schools.

This level of collaboration is not bad. It's certainly a start. But when teachers collaborate in response to top-down mandates, the creative, status-quo challenging work necessary to ensure the academic success of all disadvantaged children seldom takes place. That happens exclusively at schools that have exceptional systems of collaboration.

How can you tell if your system for collaboration is only average? The following are characteristics of average collaboration:

- There is no written document outlining why collaboration must take place, when it will take place, what will happen during collaboration meetings, and what common group norms will ensure that meetings are effective and focused.

- Grade-level meetings may be regularly or occasionally scheduled, but they are often cancelled because some teachers don't see a real need to meet.

- Meeting discussions tend to revolve around school business or classroom issues rather than strategies to ensure the academic achievement of every student.

- Teachers occasionally find reasons to miss scheduled meetings, particularly if meetings are held before or after school. Missing these meetings is not considered a violation of agreed-to norms.

If these characteristics sound familiar, there is work ahead for your school. You will need to honestly confront status quo beliefs and practices and then gather together to create an exceptional system of collaboration.

EXCEPTIONAL COLLABORATION

When a staff is on fire and committed to finding answers to the many challenges their students present, they are ready to create an exceptional system for collaboration. Doing so will give them the basic tool they need to attack other challenges they encounter every day.

What can one expect to find in an exceptional system for collaboration? That depends — every exceptional system will be unique to the school that created it. However, to help jumpstart the process we will share several questions staff members often ask when developing their exceptional systems for collaboration.

WHY ARE WE SO RESOLVED?

It is critical that a staff put in writing what they believe about the potential of every student and what they are willing to do to make the achievement of their students a reality. This speaks to the sacred responsibilities exceptional educators feel to their students. This obligation is best expressed as a "Big, Hairy, Audacious Goal," or BHAG. This BHAG clearly states the goal that can only be achieved if a staff embraces a formal system for collaboration. A BHAG is too big for one individual or a few to accomplish. It must be a team effort, driven by passionate collaboration.

A BHAG is a bold (some might say crazy) commitment by a teaching staff that describes what they are committed to accomplish. Different staffs will develop different BHAGs, but the key is for this commitment to be so big, so hairy, and so audacious that with a lot of luck and even more hard work, there may still only be a fifty percent chance of success after twenty or more years.

At Los Peñasquitos Elementary School, the teachers created a BHAG in 1996 that still guides every decision that is made and ever dollar that is spent. The staff has not yet reached this goal, but they're getting closer. At the time of this writing, they've been working at it for twelve years, and they expect to still be working at it in another twelve years. The Los Peñasquitos BHAG is as follows: Every student, without exception and without excuse, will be academically proficient in the core academic areas of reading, writing and math. This responsibility is ours.

Of course, the collaboration commitment will have additional verbiage about the responsibility a staff feels to its students, but the core will be expressed as a BHAG. Having your BHAG prominently placed at the beginning of the written collaboration plan will serve as a reminder to everyone as to why this process must never be taken lightly.

When Will Collaboration Take Place?

We like to think of collaboration as taking place according to a three-tiered model:

1. Daily Collaboration

2. Weekly Collaboration

3. Monthly Collaboration

The collaborative activities at each of these tiers are different.

Daily collaboration is generally informal. Teachers have conversations with each other about schedules, supplies, lesson coordination, and challenges they face with specific students. These are the informal conversations that teachers have had for as long as there have been schools, and they are essential for addressing the myriad of day-to-day issues that arise.

Weekly collaboration is more formal. It is common for grade-level teams to have established meetings each week where they discuss issues directly related to the academic success of each of their students. The best functioning and most successful teams limit these meetings to conversations about curriculum and practices that are directly related to student achievement. They understand that their time is too precious to use these meetings for anything other than the urgent issue of student achievement. It is important that teams set their own agendas for their weekly collaboration. We contend that the role of principals is not to set agendas for these meetings but rather to set expectations for their outcomes.

Principals at extraordinary schools empower teaching teams to be responsible for developing strategies that ensure the academic success of their students and then trust their teachers to convert those strategies into action. As long as they get results (and this is a key qualifier), teachers should never be micromanaged. Instead, their principal should support them and clear away any roadblocks.

Monthly collaboration is even more formal because these are opportunities for larger groups of teachers to engage in staff development or have conversations that involve colleagues from other grade-level teams. Vertical collaboration (when two or more contiguous teams of teachers meet, such as teachers from the second and third grade teams) is a common activity for these monthly meetings. Topics for vertical collaboration are usually decided by teachers at the end of the previous school year. Regardless of how these monthly collaboration meetings are structured, they are extremely important for ensuring consistent practice and belief among an entire staff.

It is sometimes a challenge to find time in the master calendar to schedule monthly collaboration. Every school is different, and finding this time becomes in itself an exercise in collaboration. One school created what they call Tuesday Collaboration. Every Tuesday, one hour before the children are dismissed, the school counselor, two instructional aides, and occasionally the principal take the students from two contiguous grade levels and engage them in an appropriate lesson or activity. While students are otherwise occupied, teachers meet to discuss issues related to their shared responsibilities. For instance, on one Tuesday all the fourth and fifth grade teachers may gather to align their writing rubrics. The Tuesday Collaboration model is brilliant because it is simple, effective, and free. A sample of a Tuesday Collaboration Master Schedule can be found in Appendix B.

How Will We Prepare for Meetings?

Even though a school's BHAG creates a global understanding of what teachers need to focus on during collaboration, other more specific issues need to be addressed in anticipation of actual meetings. First, the time and location of the meeting need to be shared. Also, an agenda needs to be created. Creating agendas take time, and some teams are tempted to skip this step. That is always a mistake. An agenda helps a team to focus on what is important. We are all social people and it's easy to fill a block of time with friendly conversation and stories that do not directly relate to the issues at hand. Agendas help us avoid those temptations. These steps seem so simple as to almost not be worth mentioning, but when they are neglected, collaboration meetings are much less effective.

How Will Teachers Be Involved?

First and foremost, teachers agree to participate fully in all formal collaboration activities. It is a priority for teachers to honor these times that are set aside for collaboration because this is the time they and their colleagues grapple with critical issues. Grading tests, hanging bulletin boards, and making copies never take priority over scheduled collaboration meetings.

Explicit meeting norms that describe how the teachers will engage in collaboration are established, agreed to, and written down. These norms may state, for example, that everyone will arrive on time, stay on topic, reduce outside distractions, participate fully, and end the meeting when scheduled. Whatever norms the teachers decide upon, the important point is that they agree how they will participate and that they will follow through with commitments they make.

Creating action plans can be problematic. Ask yourself if this sounds familiar. A meeting is held, ideas are shared, general understandings are reached, pleasantries are exchanged, and the meeting is adjourned. But no action plan is developed! Don't omit this key step. Agree in writing as to what needs to be done, who agrees to do it, and when it will be completed. It might be a good idea to share the action plan with your principal so he will also be in the loop.

Being respectful of time is fundamental to a well-functioning team. To do so helps teachers live balanced lives outside of school. We all know that work can expand to fill any available block of time. When collaboration meetings start and end on time, have clearly developed agendas, meeting norms, and action plans, the important work at school gets done and teachers can get on with their lives outside of school.

CAN WE BE CANDID WITH EACH OTHER?

Candid collaboration is an idea that's easy to embrace but difficult to accomplish because it requires people to confront others when necessary, and that's never easy. The culture of public schools is such that teachers rarely engage their colleagues with concerns. As principals, the authors have heard countless requests from teachers to intervene in issues that were best resolved by teachers themselves. That is a problem.

to work effectively with each other, they need to
nmunicate about common expectations. When
:tations are met, that needs to be shared. When
u⌐ey are not met, that also needs to be shared.

This is where problems usually begin. Paying compliments is easy. Talking about problems is not. The candid collaboration model works because when teachers develop and endorse this model, they have "permission" to act according to its provisions.

These are the steps we suggest for candid collaboration:

1. Support

2. Accountability

3. Intervention

4. Resource

When faced with a potential conflict, the first step is support. It is important for the staff member who is concerned to try to understand the other person's situation and support her colleague as best she can. This support will be unique to each circumstance. It may be as simple as providing a listening ear, or it may involve helping a colleague learn different strategies for remembering to show up to recess duty on time.

If the first step is not successful, the teacher moves to step 2, accountability. She holds a formal, one-on-one conversation with the colleague and directly states the concern. Doing so is not easy, and when the process breaks down, this is where it usually happens. But teachers are gentle people, and most of them intuitively know how to have these delicate conversations. When colleagues are approached kindly and appropriately, it is very common for misunderstandings to be cleared up and issues resolved.

Unfortunately, however, that is not always the case. This is when teachers move to step 3, intervention. The entire team sits down with the individual who is out of step with the others and attempts to find common interests and an appropriate resolution. If everyone involved in the process is in accord about their responsibilities to students and each other, a mutually acceptable agreement will be reached.

In rare situations where a conflict still exists even after moving through the first three steps of candid collaboration, the problem moves to step 4, resource, and the principal is requested to intervene on behalf of the team.

Candid collaboration is not only effective for resolving differences, it builds professional relationships. What better way to build professional relationships than to honestly sit down with a colleague and figure out how each can work together more successfully on behalf of children?

For candid collaboration to be truly embraced by a staff, the principal must first provide formal training. This training will not only provide skills necessary to communicate candidly, but it will also give staff members permission to do so.

COLLABORATION IN ACTION

At the beginning of the 2007 school year, a group of first grade teachers approached us with a problem. How they addressed this challenge demonstrated a clear understanding of the responsibility they felt toward their students, an appropriate use of collaboration meetings, and a willingness to engage in a candid conversation with their principals.

At Los Peñasquitos Elementary School, there is a clear expectation that all students will be proficient readers by the end of first grade. The first grade team took this responsibility very seriously. Has there ever been a year when every student achieved proficiency by the end of first grade? No. But that didn't stop each teacher on the team from believing and struggling every day as if each student would. Funds that had previously been available to pay for credentialed, part-time intervention teachers to assist in providing academic interventions were no longer available. It seemed unfair to these first grade teachers that they were still expected to ensure that each of their students were proficient readers by the end of first grade, even after the resources they had previously relied upon were gone.

After meeting with us and expressing their frustrations, three facts emerged. The first was that every student was still expected to be proficient in reading by the end of first grade. The second was that there was still no money to pay for outside academic interventions. The third was that the first grade team would have to come up with a solution that was both effective and free. Those were the brutal facts.

To their enduring credit, the first grade team never wavered in their commitment that every student would be proficient in reading. They just rolled up their sleeves and went to work. These teachers knew what they had to accomplish, and they knew the limits of their resources. What evolved was not unique, but it was nonetheless inspired. It was courageous.

The team completely restructured how they addressed the academic needs of their students. They first agreed that every teacher would be responsible for every child in first grade, which meant that they would also teach children from other classrooms. That was a profound shift in thinking and practice, and it was risky. It not only meant that their scope of responsibility expanded significantly, but also that they now had to trust their colleagues to be as effective with their own students as they were themselves. Control is never easy to give up. The teachers then aligned their schedules and grouped children across classrooms according to performance levels. They also figured out how to differentiate the amount of time made available to each student for direct reading instruction.

Because the teachers worked as a team to address the challenge of increasing student performance with decreasing resources, the following year's first grade students were more successful than students had been in the past. The irony of this story is that having no money forced this team to find a solution that was even more effective than their previous approach.

Think about what happened. A team of teachers had their backs against the wall. They were absolutely committed to the academic achievement of each of their students, but the money they had previously relied upon to get those results had been taken away. They did not say, "Forget it. If the principal can't give us what we need, then we can't produce what he wants." Instead, they buckled down and worked collaboratively to come up with a solution that was different, more effective, and free. These teachers solved their problem because they rejected excuses, they were committed to their students' success, they trusted each other, and because they believed they could find answers to this challenging problem by working together.

Exceptional collaboration is a crucial system that needs to be in place at any school that aspires to excellence. When teachers work together with the single-minded commitment that every disadvantaged child will be academically proficient, their students will be well on their way to crushing negative stereotypes and achieving the American dream.

CHAPTER SUMMARY

Teacher Collaboration

KEY POINTS

- Before a staff will willingly and enthusiastically create an exceptional system for collaboration, they must first feel an overwhelming sense of urgency for the academic proficiency of every student.

- Signs that indicate average or mediocre collaboration include:

  a. There is no written document that outlines why collaboration must take place, when it will take place, what will happen during collaboration meetings, and what common group norms will be respected by the teams.

  b. Formal, consistent teacher collaboration is not generally considered to be essential to the academic achievement of underrepresented students.

  c. Grade-level meetings may be regularly or occasionally scheduled, but they are often cancelled because no one sees a real need to meet.

  d. At meetings that do take place, discussions tend to revolve around school business or classroom issues rather than strategies to ensure the academic achievement of every student.

  e. Teachers occasionally find reasons to miss scheduled meetings, and missing these meetings is not considered a violation of agreed-to norms.

- Several simple, guiding questions are almost always asked by staffs as they create their own exceptional system for collaboration:

  a. Why are we so resolved?

  b. When will collaboration take place?

  c. How will we prepare for meetings?

  d. How will teachers be involved?

  e. Can we be candid with each other?

C H A P T E R
5

Classroom Lessons Aligned to Academic Standards

It's not enough that we do our best; sometimes we have to do what's required.

Sir Winston Churchill

Years ago when Jeff's wife was a new fourth grade teacher, she joined a team that was fixated on penguins. Their students studied every aspect of penguin life. They did penguin math and wrote penguin poetry. They performed penguin plays and rocked out to penguin dancing. They ate penguin soup (okay, that's an exaggeration).

In the evenings, often while eating dinner, Jeff learned that penguins live at the South Pole and not the North. Jeff learned that there are at least seventeen different species of penguins (and he used to be able to name most of them), that penguins bounce (not walk), and that male and female penguins share the job of sitting on eggs. His knowledge of penguins was tiny compared to that of his wife's students because her penguin unit lasted for months.

Yes, there were probably good reasons for teaching this very long penguin unit. No doubt the kids had opportunities to become better writers, and they probably integrated penguin math into their school day. The problem wasn't thematic instruction or in-depth learning about penguins. It's just that twenty-one years ago, teachers and schools were much less accountable for ensuring that every child was academically proficient in the core academic areas.

During those years, teachers had much more freedom to design lessons that were engaging and fun, without worrying that the content of their lessons may not directly help students become proficient in topics identified by the academic standards. In those days, Jeff's wife didn't feel the pressure of universal academic proficiency, but she does today. The world has changed.

AVERAGE ALIGNMENT OF LESSONS TO ACADEMIC STANDARDS

The endless penguin unit is an example of curriculum that is designed with little or no attention to academic standards. Some teachers across America still resist accepting that their primary obligation is to ensure that every student is academically proficient in the subject areas outlined by their states' academic standards. As a result, their classroom lessons have only average, and sometimes accidental, alignment with academic standards.

There are many reasons for teachers' reluctance to carefully align their curriculum to academic standards. Some teachers are convinced that they understand the academic needs of their students better than state education officials. Others have taught specific units of instruction for years, and they can't imagine not doing so in the future. Still others fear that being forced to align classroom lessons to academic standards would chip away at what they perceive to be their rights as classroom teachers to design lessons that are both engaging and appropriate. Whether teachers strongly support academic standards or bristle at the concept, most will agree that designing lessons around standards has now become a professional obligation.

Teachers usually begin this work cautiously because the task is huge. It requires new lessons to be written and old lessons to be revised. This is big, important work, and it represents a major shift for teachers in how instruction is planned and delivered.

The work of aligning classroom lessons to academic standards typically begins with a mandate from the principal, and in the beginning it is common for teachers to go through the motions of comparing their taught curriculum with academic standards without really understanding or embracing the underlying benefits for doing so.

This is not necessarily bad. As discussed previously, practices usually shift before beliefs change. An eventual understanding of the benefits of curriculum alignment comes only after teachers have experienced its direct and positive impact on academic achievement. However, once teachers see the pride in their students' eyes as they break through previously insurmountable academic barriers, their attitudes about the value of curriculum alignment will change. Until then, many teachers will grudgingly grind through the process, and the principal (who is typically the driving force) will be handed documents that describe some degree of curriculum alignment.

Schools that have average curriculum alignment usually stop here. Teachers will have gained an awareness of what is expected by going through the process of comparing standards to their current lessons, and that is good. But if teachers don't truly buy into the need to align and implement these standards, the written documents they produce may end up in file cabinet drawers, and their practices will be largely unchanged.

Does this describe the experiences at your school? If so, don't be discouraged. You are on the road to creating a culture that embraces the alignment of classroom lessons and academic standards. Now, let's get closer to your destination.

Exceptional Alignment of Lessons to Academic Standards

If your school has been following the model suggested in this book, the principal and teachers now believe that all students can be academically proficient and that the school, to a very large degree, has the power to make that happen. They understand the TurnAround Schools model for creating exceptional systems, and they have negotiated a clear understanding with each other about how they will collaborate with a focused and clear purpose.

When a staff arrives at this point together, they are ready to take on their next big challenge — aligning all classroom lessons to state academic standards, and then enthusiastically following that plan.

It is critical to begin this process with the end in mind. Principals, invite your teachers to visualize their professional lives if their teams worked together to create common classroom lessons that aligned to academic standards. Ask them to visualize how this focused instruction will help their students become competent writers, proficient readers, and more skilled at mathematics. Share with them how much easier this will make it for them to design teacher-friendly and informative assessments that will help them keep their students on track to be academically proficient. Paint this as a positive picture, because it is.

Remember the TurnAround Schools Model for Creating Exceptional Systems

You can draw upon many resources to help with this process, but remember the story of Jerry Sternin and the TurnAround Schools model for creating exceptional systems that was inspired by his work. In the end, the documents that describe how your teachers align their classroom lessons to state academic standards need to be created by them. Even though the final product will probably look very much like alignment plans that exist at other schools, your teachers must know their plan is their own.

Your first task is to look for examples of excellence that exist in your building. Have any teachers or teams done an exceptional job of carefully examining their lessons and ensuring that those lessons align to the academic standards? Have they identified holes in their instruction that need to be filled with new, targeted lessons? Have they carefully considered the amount of time spent on each unit of instruction and then modified that time to reflect the relative importance of that topic? Have they created a written plan that summarizes their work?

If so, help your staff begin by learning from these examples. This can be a little tricky because some teachers don't like to be thrust into the spotlight, but their work can and should serve as models and starting points for the rest of the staff to follow.

WRITTEN FORMAT — ONE OR MANY?

One of the first questions that will be asked concerns the format of the written plans. This may seem like a small issue, but it really is significant. Visually, this curriculum plan will most likely be in the form of a timeline, broken down by grade level, academic subject, and corresponding units of instruction, with those units linked to various academic standards.

Should each team be allowed to use their own format? Should all teachers at a school agree to one common format? Of course, this decision must be made locally (remember that the TurnAround Schools model for creating exceptional systems values unique solutions), but our suggestion is that you consider the use of one common format. Doing so will make articulation between grade levels much easier, and it will reinforce with teachers how truly interdependent they are.

Once the format of alignment plans is resolved, teachers' minds will be free and they will be more comfortable digging in and getting to work.

Rolling Up Your Sleeves and Getting to Work

Now it's time to get started. This section has some commonsense leadership tips for creating a practical product that will inspire teachers and teams and will guide them in the planning of focused, standards-based instruction.

The principal's job is to be a leader among equals. His responsibility is to set the vision, define the end product, and support the process. It is important that he makes it clear that aligning classroom lessons to academic standards falls under the 'non-negotiable' category. What needs to be done will not be open to debate. How it should be done is something that must be decided by the collective wisdom of everyone.

When supporting the process, the principal has five main responsibilities. These are to:

- Lead
- Encourage
- Drive
- Support
- Follow-up

In a healthy school environment, teachers look to their principal for leadership. When beginning the formal process of curriculum alignment, the principal must first gather teachers together and come to a common understanding about the need for curriculum alignment and the process by which it will take place. Discussions need to be held and agreements made concerning the format of the written document. Time blocks for teams to work together need to be identified, and the principal must commit to keeping these blocks of time sacred. A timeline for completion needs to be established. Each of these must be negotiated with teachers, and the principal is responsible for providing that leadership.

The principal is in the unique position to encourage teachers as they do this work. This is where previously earned good will between the principal and teachers make the process run more smoothly. As the principal acknowledges the hard work of teachers, both privately and publicly, morale will remain high.

In addition to providing encouragement, the principal must also be relentless in driving the process. You can expect oblique efforts by some teachers to weaken or water down the intensity of the project. This is understandable because curriculum alignment is hard work, and it's threatening to the status quo. The principal must resist any tendencies to slither toward mediocrity, continue to preach the gospel of excellence, push everyone to meet agreed-to deadlines, and keep this project on the front burner.

Along the way and at every step, teachers need to know they are supported. If they understand that everyone is in this together and know that their principal is committed to marching alongside, they will be much happier and more productive. The principal can show support by protecting the time that has been identified for doing this work, and by continually asking with all sincerity, "What else can I do to help?" and then by following through.

At the agreed-to completion date, the alignment plans will be written and implementation will begin — and yet the work will only have started. Everyone should understand that these written plans must be in a constant state of review and revision. The principal can keep the conversations going by making curriculum alignment a recurring topic at staff meetings, by meeting with individual teams and reviewing how their common lessons align with the academic standards, and by observing the instruction of teachers and having subsequent conversations about the alignment of the lessons that were observed.

As mentioned before, aligning curriculum to academic standards is hard work. It requires teachers who are courageous and committed, who really dig into the standards, and who are brave enough to change their taught curriculum as necessary. It also requires a principal who is tenacious, supportive, and absolutely committed to the critical importance of curriculum alignment.

WHERE ARE YOU NOW?

Actually, at this point you're a long way down the road toward creating a school that knows no limits to the academic achievement of every child. Think about where you have traveled so far.

First, you created a culture of universal achievement. There is now a general consensus among everyone on campus that all children, regardless of the subgroup to which they are assigned, are capable of being academically proficient in the core academic areas. You also understand and believe that teachers and their principal have the resources and ability to neutralize many of the challenges that get in the way of students reaching this incredibly ambitious goal.

Then you created an exceptional system for teacher collaboration. You rejected the idea that just because teachers meet and talk, they are engaged in effective collaboration. Teachers now meet regularly with a clear purpose, and they are poised to tackle big challenges that stand in the way of their students' learning.

The next logical challenge you faced was ensuring that the taught curriculum aligned with the academic standards. Everyone worked together on this imposing project, and teams created unit and lesson plans that are clearly aligned with standards.

Now that everyone is teaching what needs to be taught, the next big question is, "What are the kids actually learning?" Finding the answer to that question is the work of the next exceptional system.

Chapter Summary

Classroom Lessons Aligned to Academic Standards

Key Points

- Follow the TurnAround Schools model for creating exceptional systems.

- Decide on a format. The authors suggest that all grade level teams adopt a consistent format.

- The principal has five main responsibilities during this process:

  a. Lead the work.

  b. Encourage teachers as they struggle collaboratively to legitimately align their classroom lessons.

  c. Drive the process! Some teachers will attempt to reduce the intensity of the project, and the principal must maintain a reasonable amount of tension.

  d. Support his teachers by continuing to ask, "What else can I do to help?"

  e. Create and implement a schedule for reviewing and revising the alignment work that was initially done. Everyone should understand that this work is never-ending.

CHAPTER

6

Classroom Assessments that Guide Instruction and Interventions

High expectations without a means of measurement are hollow.

Samuel Casey Carter

In many schools, if you want to set off an animated discussion, just bring up assessment. Many teachers are fed up with a seemingly unending series of mandated tests. There are annual state assessments that usually take several days to complete, and there are district-mandated tests that are often required at regular intervals. How many of us have heard the following, maybe a thousand times? "Test, test, test! All we ever do is test! When do they expect us to teach?"

The root of this problem is threefold:

- Information received from state tests has limited value for teachers.

- Central offices often foist student assessments on teachers with little discussion or legitimate input. All teachers are seldom brought into the conversation when assessments are selected and testing calendars are created.

- Some teachers don't understand or believe that information they receive from classroom assessments is essential to their efforts to ensure that every one of their students will be academically proficient.

Most teachers understand that administering annual state summative assessments is a fact of life, and they grit their teeth and get through it. But when teachers are forced to stop teaching, if only temporarily, to give top-down mandated district tests without having been involved in any serious discussions about their appropriateness or applicability, they are naturally resistant. This response is completely rational and understandable, and in our opinion, is the reason why teachers so often resent district mandated testing.

Assessments generally fall into two categories — summative and classroom. This distinction is important because teachers generally find summative assessments to be of limited value and certain classroom assessments of their own choosing to be extremely helpful.

Summative assessments are commonly known as assessments of learning. An example would be annual state tests. These tests typically report the learning of students after the school year has ended. Some people refer to summative assessments as post mortems — they provide information after the patient has, well, moved on. When summative assessment results are received, typically in late summer, it's too late for teachers to have any influence on the learning of students who have been promoted to the next grade level. That's the main reason these assessments have limited use for teachers.

Summative assessments do have value, however, particularly for individuals who monitor programs and account for their success or who report on the performance of large groups of students. Superintendents and school boards pay close attention to summative assessments because these assessments show the direction of student-achievement trend lines.

Classroom assessments are commonly known as assessments for learning. These include any assessments that give immediate information about what individual students know or can do. Good teachers value classroom assessments tremendously because the information these assessments provide can be used by teachers to modify lessons and design appropriate academic interventions.

Classroom assessments can range from casual teacher observation or classroom quizzes to more formal, grade-level designed and commonly administered assessments. For the purpose of this chapter, we are referring to the latter.

AVERAGE USE OF CLASSROOM ASSESSMENTS

All teachers administer some types of classroom assessments although the quality of these assessments varies from teacher to teacher and from school to school. Many teachers and schools are currently at an average stage when using them.

Where the use of classroom assessments is still at the average stage, teachers are seldom involved in the selection of tests, and because of this they often feel disrespected. They really don't understand why these tests are important or how they will directly impact student achievement. Teachers at these schools have typically not been involved in determining testing frequency or testing windows. Morale is low.

Once tests have been given, teachers seldom meet voluntarily and enthusiastically as grade level teams to analyze the resulting data for the purpose of modifying their curriculum or for designing interventions. They are reluctant to involve students directly in the assessment process, and they are equally reluctant to involve parents.

Until teachers and their principal make a conscientious effort to develop an exceptional system of classroom assessments, the use of these assessments at their school is usually limited, relatively ineffective, and often the source of tension and frustration.

EXCEPTIONAL USE OF CLASSROOM ASSESSMENTS

Before teachers and administrators will welcome an exceptional system that defines their use of assessments, they must first believe that every child is capable of academic proficiency and that teachers and their principal have an uncompromising obligation to make it happen. They must also acknowledge a need for the additional information necessary to make that happen.

Once this happens, they will demand assessments that will guide their work as they pursue the academic success of every student. Teachers soon realize that without the data that comes from classroom assessments, they cannot achieve their goal of universal student achievement.

CREATING AN EXCEPTIONAL SYSTEM OF ASSESSMENTS

We believe grade-level teams of teachers should have the primary responsibility of selecting or creating their formal classroom assessments. Teachers often question the value of assessments that they perceive as having been foisted on them by offsite directors and administrators. But when teachers are respectfully given responsibility for creating their own unique and meaningful assessment system to which they will hold themselves accountable, they will be much more inclined to embrace their plan and use those assessments as they were intended. Like everyone, teachers own what they create. What could be more respectful of teachers who clearly understand and demonstrate their responsibility for student achievement than to let them direct the process of selecting their own formal, common, classroom assessments?

At the school where we were co-principals, we guided the overall process. The entire teaching staff reached consensus about the definition of classroom assessments, the need for common, regularly administered assessments, the specific curricular areas about which teachers needed data, and examples of what those assessments might look like. We continued the conversation by announcing several non-negotiables that were not open for discussion. For example, every grade-level team was expected to select meaningful, formal classroom assessments that would truly inform the instructional decisions of the team. All teachers would administer these assessments at agreed-upon times during the school year. The resulting data would then be collected, disaggregated, and shared with each teacher in a timely manner. Scheduled discussions would be held about actions that would be driven by this data. However, as with every initiative at the school, how this work proceeded was completely a function of teacher input and involvement.

SELECTION OF ASSESSMENTS

The selection of classroom assessments is critically important. The data that is derived from these assessments must be meaningful, and it must accurately measure academic competencies that are valued by teachers and reflected in the standards. But teachers and principals need to fight against the fear that they don't have the professional expertise necessary to select or create these assessments. Rarely is that true. Nobody is asking a staff to design a system that will be judged by assessment gurus or adopted by a state. Instead, they are developing their own system that will be used by teachers who are collectively responsible for the academic achievement of several hundred students. That's all.

One additional point is very important to understand. At the end of every school year, the principal must sit down with each team and ask them which assessments provided meaningful data and which did not. The team will continue to use those assessments that did, and they'll jettison those that didn't. There is nothing sacred about an initial list of assessments. Teachers should understand that the only reason they administer assessments is because those assessments provide valuable information. When that is no longer the case, they must feel free to replace those assessments with others that will potentially provide more meaningful data.

You'll find a snapshot of the assessment plan that was created by our third grade team in Appendix D. As you can see, the assessments they selected represent a reasonable cross-section of standards-based skills.

Assessment Calendar

One of the first decisions a staff must make concerns the frequency of testing. How often is enough? How often is too much? How many days should the testing window be open? The answers to these questions can only come from those who are responsible for their students' learning.

This decision will be driven primarily by the needs of teachers to acquire the data they need to form intervention groups, modify curriculum, track the progress of students, and complete progress reports. Some teachers are so data driven that they need this formal data every month, and that is perfectly appropriate. Other schools decide to balance the twin demands of instruction and assessment a little differently and assess less often. Teachers at our school agreed to administer their formal, classroom assessments three times during the school year.

The bottom line when considering the frequency of assessments is, it all depends. There is no right answer. What's essential is for teachers to meet, talk, negotiate, consider the needs of their students, create an assessment calendar, and then conscientiously follow the schedule.

Articulation Meetings — Reviewing the Data with a Bias Toward Action

After every test administration, data should be collected, disaggregated by student, and returned to grade-level teams in a user-friendly format. Then a formal articulation meeting should be held that includes the teachers, the principal, and any other staff members who have a direct impact on the achievement of these students (English Language Learner

(ELL) coordinator or aide, special education resc
teacher, intervention team leader, etc.). The purpose of ....
meeting is to review the assessment results, child by child,
and to make decisions about appropriate academic or social
interventions.

This time is devoted exclusively to considering the specific
needs of every child. Important questions are asked, and
conversations tend to be spirited. What was the child's
proficiency level at the beginning of the year? How much
progress has been made? In exactly which areas is she
struggling? What will we do to remediate those learning
challenges? When will we reevaluate her progress? What
else can we do to help her become academically proficient,
hopefully by the end of the current school year?

At this meeting the rubber meets the road. You can assess and
collect data all day and every day, but unless those activities
lead to specific actions in support of struggling learners, your
efforts will be wasted. Articulation meetings are perfect times
for all professionals who are responsible for the academic
proficiency of certain children to gather together, review
data, and decide on the specific actions necessary to move
students toward proficiency.

INVOLVING STUDENTS

If adults are the only ones to review and act upon assessments,
they are missing perhaps their greatest opportunity to
use assessment data to positively influence the academic
progress of their students. Failing to involve students is like
the executive committee at Intel getting user feedback about
chip problems and then making decisions without involving
their engineers! Intel would never be so shortsighted, and
neither should we.

Teachers who have never made the effort to involve their
students in analyzing their assessment results may fear that
this process is too time consuming or not potentially worth
the effort. Trust us, that couldn't be farther from the truth.

We know of no other assessment strategy as effective as involving students in the process.

In your quest to involve students in assessment, one of your most important tasks will be to help them understand why assessments are important and then to encourage them to actively engage in the process. When students perceive tests as being only for the benefit of their teacher, they will naturally view these assessments as just one more low-stakes interruption that must be tolerated. Your goal must be, somehow, to make assessments as important to students as they are to teachers. Assessments will become one of the major motivators that focus students' daily efforts, learning will take on a much greater meaning for students, and their academic performance will improve significantly.

How to Help Students Value Their Assessments

The following are four steps teachers can take that will help their students learn to value the assessments they are given:

1. Each grade-level team of teachers must come to a clear understanding about why they give classroom assessments and then reach a shared commitment about engaging their students in the process. The primary purpose of classroom assessments is not for assigning grades. Assessments should not be used as a hammer for strong-arming students into studying and making reasonable academic efforts. Tests should not be used as traditional time fillers (It's Friday, so it must be test day!).

   Classroom assessments should first and foremost be a way for students and teachers to see how much progress a student has made and what the next specific learning goals will be for that child. With this information, teachers will be able to design appropriate, differentiated curriculum and targeted interventions. Students will know exactly what they need to focus on, and with the right guidance, they will know which strategies are necessary to reach their next learning goals.

2. Teachers must next engage students in the ass
process by explicitly teaching students why assessr
important. Be sure students know that assessments wu..
be used as a punishment. Rather, they need to understand
that assessments will be used to help both you and them
to focus on their next academic steps.

The children must also understand how to interpret the
data — with your assistance, of course. This is simply a
matter of projecting a data report on the classroom screen,
walking the kids through what the numbers mean, and
discussing how you and they will make decisions based on
those numbers.

3. Teachers then create a class goal. This is a very powerful
way to provide a daily classroom focus on the one area of
the curriculum that needs the greatest attention. It's really
a great exercise to go through with the kids.

First, project the overall class assessment data for all the
children to see. This data will most likely include the
results of several assessments covering different areas of
the curriculum. Then lead your class in some self-discovery.
"Let's try to figure out what this means. Who can explain
these first results? How about the second?" At a certain
point, your students will have a general understanding
about what the results mean and about the overall academic
strengths and weaknesses of the class. It should be easy
for students to identify the area where they scored lowest
and where their greatest future efforts are required.

After students understand what the data mean, they are
ready for the most powerful part of this exercise. You will
all agree on one class goal that will be in place for a specific
period of time — typically until the next formal assessment
administration. For instance, the class goal may be in the
area of reading comprehension. When crafting the goal
with students, be sure it is stated as a performance goal.
For instance, let's say seven out of twenty students initially
met a certain benchmark number. The class goal could be

for fifteen students to meet this benchmark number after the next test administration.

It is important not only to negotiate a class goal but also to agree on several strategies that students can individually and collectively use to meet this goal. For example, if reading comprehension is the class goal, your strategies may include the following:

- We will use Venn diagrams to learn about similarities and differences between things we will be reading about.

- Our teacher will create several true and false statements about the topic we are reading, and we will predict which of these are true and which are false. When we read, we'll find out if we were right.

- We will complete a KWL chart (already know — want to know — what we learned) before and after some of our reading assignments.

This class goal and these strategies should be posted prominently in the classroom (often on a large sheet of butcher paper) and referred to often. By doing this, the importance of reading comprehension will be kept at the forefront of everyone's mind. When the next assessment window arrives, your students will be anxious to find out if they met their class goal. Creating class goals and their accompanying strategies is brilliant, it is motivating, and it works.

4. Finally, teachers and students negotiate individual student goals. The process for doing so is similar to creating a class goal.

The teacher and each individual student sit down together and briefly review the student's assessment results. They then agree on the one area of greatest need and identify three specific strategies that the child will use to make significant progress in this area. This goal and the strategies are then recorded on a form. A sample Student Goals Form can be found in Appendix C.

Teachers often make a collage on a classroom wall comprised of every student's individual goals. Having their goals publicly displayed is a source of pride for students. The children also transfer their goals and strategies to a notebook-sized form provided by their teacher, and that form is then placed at the front of their three-ring binders. Having their goals displayed on the classroom wall and placed at the front of their binders means they are always in front of the students.

Children are also expected to memorize their goal and strategies. When we walked down the hallway at school and encountered a child, we often asked, "What's your student goal?" Almost always, the child would immediately tell us his goal and what strategies he would use to reach that goal.

The most encouraging aspect of class and student goals is that, almost without exception, students see their greatest academic growth in the areas represented by their class and student goals. This applies equally to gifted students and those who struggle academically.

INVOLVING PARENTS

Initially when Jeff was principal at Los Peñasquitos Elementary School, the teachers were not willing to focus on academic results. Good enough was good enough, and those folks weren't motivated to drive for better student performance.

Jeff was at a loss as to how he could encourage rapid results. Public school principals have some ability to influence the practices of teachers, particularly if teachers and the principal respect each other. But change came slowly, and his students didn't have any extra time. Every day was important, and those days could never be recaptured.

Jeff had an idea. What if he merged individual student data into letters that also showed class averages and mailed those letters directly to parents? His guess was that this new information would shock many parents, and that they would bypass him and have direct conversations with their children's teachers concerning what everyone needed to do to improve their children's academic performance.

That is exactly what parents did, and this turned out to be a very effective way to involve parents. They learned exactly what they and their children needed to do for their children to be more successful, and teachers were suddenly much more accountable to parents for their children's academic success.

It should not be surprising that the teachers were initially skeptical of this new openness. Accountability can be an unforgiving taskmaster. But the open sharing of data gradually began to appeal to teachers, and it eventually became part of how we did business. If student achievement at Los Peñasquitos Elementary School was going to be our number one goal, our performance must be transparent, and we must be willing to learn and improve based upon that performance. That went for teachers, and for students.

Jeff learned an important lesson in those early years. If we are to expect parents to help their children reach their academic potential, the parents must have direct and immediate knowledge of their children's assessment results.

Classroom assessments are at the center of student achievement. Once teachers and their principal work together to develop this exceptional system, and after they experience the power of this tool for helping them and their students define and focus their work, they will never look back. Simply put, neither teachers nor students can reach their potential without enthusiastically using classroom assessments.

CHAPTER SUMMARY

Classroom Assessments that Drive Instruction and Interventions

KEY POINTS

- Summative assessments are assessments of learning. The results of summative assessments are typically received after the end of the school year. These assessments are valued most often by district office administrators and boards of education who have global responsibility for monitoring student achievement trends.

- Classroom assessments are assessments for learning. These are most valued by teachers because they give immediate information about the learning needs of individual students.

- Teachers are too often not involved in the design, scheduling, and managing of classroom assessments. This commonly results in resentment and a natural resistance to what is perceived as top-down, imposed, classroom assessments. Teachers should always be very involved in the following ways:

  a. selecting classroom assessments that will be used by the school and their individual grade level teams

  b. creating an assessment calendar

  c. meeting together after each test administration to review the data with a bias toward making decisions about appropriate academic and social interventions

d. involving students in the assessment process

e. sharing data with parents

- The assessment plan should be reviewed at the end of each school year. Assessments that are not effective must be eliminated and replaced by other assessments that have the potential to produce better information about the specific achievement levels of individual students.

CHAPTER

7

A System for Easily Managing Data

The most commonly spoken language at a school should be the language of data.

Damen Lopez

Classroom assessments generate data. In fact, generating data is really the only legitimate motivation for giving assessments to students. Data provides information about the academic strengths and weaknesses of children, and data directs our responses when students are not on track to meet or exceed standards of proficiency. Of all the languages represented on a campus, it is data that should be spoken most often and most fluently.

AVERAGE USE OF DATA MANAGEMENT

Data management is commonly addressed by schools and districts, but we still find many instances where schools rely on rudimentary and relatively ineffective means to manage the data generated by commonly administered classroom assessments.

While waiting for data management systems to be fully developed, data is often compiled and handwritten, or word-processed, into static documents. These reports may provide support for an initial conversation or two, but they often end up in file drawers or folders, never to be seen again. Data managed this way is interactive only if someone pulls the paper out of the drawer or accesses the document on a computer. It is not dynamic, and it does not lend itself to disaggregation or the longitudinal slicing-and-dicing that educators eventually demand as they become more demanding about determining the specific learning needs of their students.

You can argue that this elementary means of managing data is better than nothing, and you would be right. But as teachers and administrators begin to realize the untapped power of classroom assessments, they will soon demand data analysis tools that are much more powerful.

Exceptional Use of Data Management

In the early days of the revolution at Los Peñasquitos Elementary School, we had no means to effectively manage assessment data, even though grade-level teams of teachers were well on their way to embracing classroom assessments. Assessment was all we talked about and just as morning follows night, our teachers began to demand a means to more easily manage the data that started to flow.

Jeff went to the district office for help. To the best of his ability he pleaded his case, but the only help the superintendent and his assistants offered was a vague assurance that they were "working on a software solution." Jeff asked if that "software solution" would allow us to enter site-specific data. They wrinkled their brows, hesitated, and then said yes, but he knew they had no idea what they were talking about. Against his better judgment, he waited, and waited, and waited.

During the next year we became increasingly frustrated because the district didn't communicate a sense of urgency about creating this new system for managing data. Even if they did eventually roll out a solution (they did), we had no confidence that it would be flexible enough to allow us to enter our own site data (it wasn't).

Jeff eventually woke up one morning and realized that nobody cared more about the success of Los Pen's students than we did, and if this problem were to be solved it would have to be solved by us. This maverick approach had served us well before, and it would serve us well again.

The answer to the data management challenge turned out to be pretty simple. Jeff was convinced we could find a local programmer to design an assessment database using a program called Microsoft Access. Jeff had a small amount of money to pay for its development, and one of our clerks was eager to enter and export the data after it was built.

A local freelance Access programmer was recommended, and Jeff scheduled a meeting with him and a few teachers who were unusually analytical and who had clear visions about what this database needed to do. We all sat down together around a chalkboard and developed a set of software specifications. Jeff dipped into a donation account and paid the programmer five hundred dollars (Remember, this was several years ago!), and six weeks later we were in business.

That's about how easy it was. We had a problem that needed to be fixed. No one was willing to solve our problem for us. We found effective models in other similar schools. We used the resources at hand ($500, a team of intuitive, analytical teachers, a clerk who was willing and able to import and export data, and a local freelance programmer), and created our own solution. Today, ten years later, Los Peñasquitos still uses that same database. Knowing that we did it ourselves, based upon our unique needs, when no one else would help, made it all the more sweet.

Creating Your Own Database

If you decide to create your own software-based data management solution, remember that its initial design will be critical to its success. If the following criteria are considered at the beginning of the project, you'll have a good chance of creating a system that will serve your teachers well for years:

- New data fields must be easy to create.

- Data must be easy to enter.

- Customizable reports must be easy to build.

- Reports must easily show growth over time.

- Reports must be easily understood by teachers.

New Data Fields Must Be Easy to Create

One of the core values of a school's assessment system is the understanding that teachers should stop using assessments that are not effective and adopt new assessments that better serve their needs. This flexibility in program creates the need for an equivalent flexibility in a data management system, and new data fields should be easy to add.

Data Must Be Easy to Enter

Systems that fail are systems that are more trouble than they're worth. Systems that succeed are easy to use, do what they're supposed to do, and don't cause frustration. Those should be the goals of your new database, and the first step toward meeting those goals is to make sure data is easy to enter.

Ease of entry begins with selecting assessments that generate specific types of data. Databases do really well at tracking numbers and categories, and assessments need to generate one or the other. For instance, if a child performed at a Running Record level 22, or if her fluency rate was 110, those numbers could be easily entered into a database. If a child took the CELDT test and scored at the early intermediate level, that would be an appropriate category to report. On the other hand, anecdotal observations similar to comments found on progress reports do not work in databases. "Benjamin is making reasonable efforts, but he continues to have difficulty applying problem solving skills to real-world applications" is important information to have, but information in this form is not appropriate for entry into a database.

Once assessments have been given and scored, teachers must report the results to the data entry clerk in a manner that allows for easy entry and minimal chances for error. We found it helpful for grade-level teams to fill out simple forms that listed students alphabetically, the test they were given, and their individual scores. That way the data clerk only had to scroll from student to student entering numbers into the correct data fields, reducing possibilities for error and making her work go much faster.

Customizable Reports Must Be Easy to Build

Last year, a teacher came to our office to talk with us about a grant opportunity she was interested in pursuing. One proposal requirement mandated that she disaggregate and report detailed information about the reading achievement of our Hispanic students — boys versus girls, Hispanic versus Caucasian, various data trends, and so on. To gather this information by hand would have taken hours and quite honestly may have never been done. But once we clearly understood which data were required, we merely sat down with our data clerk and explained our needs. She applied the appropriate filters and within about thirty minutes we had a customized report with the exact data we needed.

That's how easily data reports should be to create. Of course, as mentioned previously, the means to do this must be designed into the system at its creation. For those of us who are not programmers, it all seems a bit mystical. But for programmers, it's just another day at work.

REPORTS MUST EASILY SHOW GROWTH OVER TIME

There is an old saying among statisticians that it takes at least three data points to show a trend. For instance, if this month Dorothy scored 80 percent on a math assessment, you would have no data whatsoever to indicate a performance trend since you have no idea how she performed in the past. But if she also scored 65 percent the month before on a related assessment, you may be tempted to infer a trend. That would be a mistake. All you have are two data points, which is not enough. Either one of those tests could indicate a "bad test day" or a day when Dorothy guessed particularly well. However, if three months ago she also took a related test and scored 55 percent, you would then have three data points — 55, 65, and 80 — and could say that there appears to be an improving trend in Dorothy's math achievement. That would be great information to have because it would indicate that whatever was being done (by the teachers and by Dorothy) was working.

A properly designed database will easily allow you to compare assessment results over time and show whether or not trend lines exist. This is a powerful benefit of a well-designed database.

REPORTS MUST BE EASILY UNDERSTOOD BY TEACHERS

In the end, what really matters is for teachers to receive a summary of individual and group performance in a timely manner and that the report be complete and easy to understand. If that doesn't happen, all your efforts will have been wasted because the data will be ignored. Remember that successful systems do what they're supposed to do and don't cause frustration, and the last people you want to frustrate are teachers.

It is imperative that a representative group of teachers meet during the design phase to discuss report formats. This group will decide on report layouts for various purposes that are simple for teachers to follow. The programmer will then design "canned" reports that will be easy to populate. Of course, a competent data entry clerk will not be limited to these canned reports and will be able to use the capabilities of Microsoft® Office Access to create customized reports that accommodate specific or unusual requests.

As we reflect upon what is required to create an exceptional system for managing data, we're struck by the linear nature of this project. We believe it falls to the principal to first gather the leadership team together and create an outline of the specific steps that need to be taken. Many ideas for doing so can be gleaned from this chapter. Once that is done, the work needs to be accomplished one step after another. In a reasonable period of time, the staff will have their own, unique system for managing assessment data, and if it is set up correctly, it will exceed their reasonable expectations.

Chapter Summary

A System for Easily Managing Data

Key Points

- If your school or district does not have the means to easily and effectively manage data, hire a freelance programmer to create a unique database for your school.

- It is critical at the design stage to include the following capabilities in the database:

  a. New data fields must be easy to create.

  b. Data must be easy to enter.

  c. Customizable reports must be easy to build.

  d. Reports must easily show growth over time.

  e. Reports must be easily understood by teachers.

C H A P T E R
8

Data-Driven Interventions, Both Academic and Social

*Sometimes our light goes out
but is blown into flame by another human being.*

Albert Schweitzer

Ten years ago we knew we wanted our delightful but struggling students to be the most academically successful children in our large, affluent, high-achieving school district. For them to do so we knew we needed to intervene when they weren't on track to be academically proficient. We stumbled in the dark, looking for strategies that had the potential to make that improbable hope come true. During those early years, we never considered the TurnAround Schools model for developing exceptional systems. We weren't aware of any comparable schools that had created intervention models we could emulate. All we had in those days were dreams, boundless energy, sheer determination, and an abundance of confidence that perhaps, maybe, just possibly bordered on arrogance (or so we were told).

We used to admit that our only real strategy for igniting this educational revolution was to throw ten ideas against the wall and hope that one would stick. Our brute-force efforts were primitive, and we suffered many more failures than success. But that never slowed us down because there were those inevitable small successes that kept us going. Jeff had read Michael Schmoker's book *Results* in which Schmoker claimed that quick, small wins could keep the enthusiasm of teachers alive. Schmoker was correct.

Average Implementation of Academic and Social Interventions

As we experienced those early struggles, we learned from them. Where we were ten years ago, struggling desperately to find intervention strategies that really showed results, is where many schools are today. After working with hundreds of schools, we believe the most common characteristics of schools that struggle to develop an exceptional intervention system are:

- The staff does not approach the development of an exceptional system for intervention in a formal, deliberate, systematic manner.

- No written intervention plan has been thoughtfully negotiated by the entire staff.

- The effectiveness of current interventions are not continually evaluated with the understanding that if they aren't working as expected, they will be stopped and new strategies will be found.

Schools that struggle to develop an exceptional intervention system often have a few interventions in place that aren't very effective. Let us share a few examples that illustrate this point.

Are Impact Teachers Having
an Impact on Learning?

Last year, we worked with an elementary school staff that had a logical plan for helping their struggling students, but the way they implemented that plan failed to get results. This school had a significant amount of Title 1 money, much of which they used to hire part-time, credentialed teachers for the purpose of working with small groups of children who struggled in the core academic areas. These part-time folks were called impact teachers.

Classroom teachers would meet and identify their most struggling students by areas of greatest weakness — math, reading, or writing. Some children received all three labels. The children were then formed into small groups and met with impact teachers during the daily afternoon intervention block.

Conventional wisdom argued that the real value of impact teachers was their ability to provide focused instruction to small groups of children that had similar needs. In theory it sounded reasonable. But in practice things did not go so well. Impact teachers were hired to supplement classroom lessons, which they sometimes did, but more often they provided primary instruction. They were supervised poorly, and communication between them and their students' teachers was irregular. The children continued to struggle. What we found most interesting was how the system responded to this situation. It didn't. The problem continued for years without change. Why was that?

First, we think an overworked principal and teachers who rarely carved out time to meet together just assumed they were doing the right thing for their students and that everything was going well. After all, it made sense for credentialed teachers to focus on the specific needs of only a few students, right?

Second, the staff believed it was providing targeted interventions by qualified teachers, and if the kids still weren't learning, perhaps they weren't trying hard enough, or maybe they just weren't developmentally prepared for the material. Either way, it made sense to the teachers and principal to continue the current model in hopes that eventually the kids would step up their game.

Third, and this is a bit touchy, but the truth is that a few teachers were secretly glad to have someone else be responsible for these struggling students. It's human nature to avoid challenging situations where the probability of success is poor, and avoiding that responsibility motivated a few of the teachers.

When we began working with this school, they had been using impact teachers in this manner for five years. That was just how business was done. The staff had never met together and honestly asked themselves, "Does the current way we use impact teachers get the results our students need?" If they had asked that question, and if they had been honest with each other, their answer would have been no.

Are They Classroom Aides or Personal Assistants?

The second example of ineffective interventions is one Jeff confronted at the beginning of the Los Peñasquitos revolution. For years, classroom aides had been hired for every teacher. As one might expect, this "intervention" was very popular. It was also very expensive. As a new principal, Jeff found it surprising that year after year the school continued to spend large amounts of money on aides even though student achievement had trailed the district consistently for twenty-six years. Where was the bang for our buck?

Jeff realized he was treading on thin ice as he began to question teachers about how they used their classroom aides. As he walked from classroom to classroom, day after day, he saw some instances where aides were helping individual students. He also observed aides running dittos, laminating papers, hanging bulletin boards, and correcting tests. Of course, it's always nice to have help, but how could we justify using limited resources to hire classroom aides who often acted as personal assistants? As Jeff had these conversations with teachers, some actually expressed a sense of panic. Aides had been part of their worlds for so long that many of them couldn't imagine doing their jobs without them. When he pointed out the obvious, that even with classroom aides their students still performed poorly, some teachers responded, "But just imagine how much worse they'll do if our aides are gone!"

This was another example of a practice that had been in place for years without ever being honestly examined for its effectiveness. In the end, Jeff felt he could justify keeping kindergarten aides, but he eliminated the others. Sometimes a principal just has to make a difficult decision, and this was one of those times. He used the money we saved to fund other interventions that teachers wanted and needed.

The following year, student achievement actually increased dramatically. This improvement was due to both the burgeoning development of a culture of universal achievement and the new interventions made possible by the money that had recently been liberated.

DOES DETENTION WORK AS AN INTERVENTION?

The third example involves efforts to modify the behavior of students by using one of the most time-honored traditions in our business — detention. The fundamental belief behind detention, one that is rarely challenged, is that punishing children who misbehave by assigning them detention will sufficiently motivate them to not misbehave in the future.

We admit that we don't have rigorous data to support our skepticism, but based upon years of personal experience and work we've done with schools across America, we don't believe for a second that detention is a generally effective intervention. We've seen too many examples where it does not work, and we bet you have also.

This is what we found. Two categories of students are typically assigned detention. First are the good kids who just made an honest mistake. These are children who usually behave responsibly, but who may not have done a homework assignment for some presumably legitimate reason or maybe forgot to have a test signed. If these children are assigned detention, it's likely that their behavior won't repeat. But it probably wouldn't have repeated anyway. So for these children, detention is a punishment, but the punishment probably won't change their future behavior.

The second category of student is those who are just behaviorally challenged. There's no other polite way to put it. These children constantly push the edges of conformity, and as a result, they have their own dedicated seats at detention. You know the type of child we mean. You can probably picture one right now. Is detention working as an intervention for her? No, it's not. Sending her to detention may provide some satisfaction for her teacher or principal or noon duty supervisor, but it's not changing her behavior.

We realized this paradox when we finally noticed that some children had detentions assigned continuously for weeks ahead, and detention wasn't changing their behavior. They just kept showing up every day, slouching into the room, sitting sullenly until the bell rang, and then continuing to make the same poor decisions. It wasn't until we were struck by the absurdity of this situation that we finally sat down one day and said, "Whoa! Let's step back and think about what's happening!" This was a difficult discussion for some because it required them to seriously examine decades of preconceived notions about how to change the behavior of students.

We concluded that changing behavior should be more about teaching and less about punishing. Some old-school folks cringed at the idea, but focusing on changing behavior worked nonetheless. (It worked spectacularly, but more about that later.) What's interesting is that it took so long for us to realize that detention did not work and also that it was so difficult for some to break with tradition by getting rid of detention and replacing it with more effective means of teaching good behavior.

In each of these examples, the staffs originally fell short in the three areas identified at the beginning of this chapter. They did not approach the development of the intervention in a deliberate and systematic manner, they had no formal, written intervention plan that was negotiated by the entire staff, and the interventions were not continually evaluated for their effectiveness.

EXCEPTIONAL IMPLEMENTATION OF ACADEMIC AND SOCIAL INTERVENTIONS

We realize we've driven this point home numerous times, but when a staff endeavors to create their own exceptional system, their work must be based on a commitment to following the TurnAround Schools model.

1. Identify an individual or a team in your school, or in a school that looks like yours, that succeeds in extraordinary and unexpected ways.

2. Identify the practices that account for their success.

3. Using your own unique resources, replicate the core principles of those practices and turn them into your own exceptional systems.

By following this process, each school's exceptional systems for intervention will look somewhat different from those found at other schools, and that is exactly as it should be.

The following intervention practices have been successfully implemented by TurnAround schools across the nation, and they can be used as springboards for conversation. Some may work at your school. Others won't. Whether they will or won't is unimportant. What is important is that you follow the TurnAround Schools model and that you start today.

Intervention on a Shoestring — The Intervention Team

As with the development of every exceptional system, necessity is the mother of invention. The teachers at Los Peñasquitos Elementary School faced the most common of dilemmas — many of the students in first through third grades were not yet proficient in reading, an extraordinary intervention was needed, and there was very little money to pay for it.

We approached this problem like we approached every other problem. We gathered together representative members of the staff and started asking questions. What is the problem? Do we know of anyone who has successfully addressed this problem? What did they do? Do we have the resources to accomplish something similar?

Here were the facts as we knew them:

- Some of our students in first, second, and third grades were not proficient in reading.

- Having students who were not reading at a proficient level was unacceptable.

- A reading specialist had been providing supplementary teaching to several small groups of students in the primary grades with notable success.

- She was using a specific research-based curriculum.

- We had four well-trained kindergarten teachers, each of whom taught half-day kindergarten, who could provide similar interventions to a much larger number of groups.

Three aspects of this developing plan were particularly attractive. First, we identified a successful model that we could emulate. Second, our primary resource was four of our own, well-trained kindergarten teachers. These teachers knew the children, and they were eager to provide them with this additional help. Third, with the exception of purchasing four small sets of curriculum, the intervention was almost free!

The first thing we did was schedule all of the following year's kindergarten classes for the morning. That allowed our newly formed Intervention Team to teach their kindergarten classes in the morning and meet with small groups of children after lunch, following the children's primary classroom literacy instruction.

We then purchased a structured curriculum for our intervention teachers. Our reading specialist had used this curriculum successfully with small groups, and we were confident it would provide the results our students needed.

We identified one of the kindergarten teachers as our Lead Intervention Teacher, paid her a small stipend, and gave her significant authority to manage this program. Doing so proved to be a very wise decision. She was extremely capable, and she was passionate about the potential for these interventions to help students become proficient readers.

The Intervention Team met every two weeks with the principals and counselor to review all aspects of the program. At this meeting, the Intervention Team Leader reported on which children were being promoted out of their groups (which happened often) and which students were being invited to join. One characteristic of these groups was the ease with which children flowed in and out. These decisions were always made on the basis of ever-present data.

When we think of all the academic interventions that contributed to the success of students at Los Peñasquitos Elementary School, no other approached the broad-based impact of our Intervention Team.

GRADE-LEVEL INTERVENTIONS

Grade-level teams of teachers should constantly be asking themselves, "What can we do differently that we haven't yet thought of?" It takes real courage for teachers to break out of their traditional thinking and consider options that at first may seem unconventional or impossible. But last year we worked with a team of fourth and fifth grade teachers who did exactly that.

This school had one fourth grade and two fifth grade classes. The three teachers worked together well, but they weren't pleased with the mediocre success of their lower performing students. Not surprisingly, the school had no money to provide additional interventions so anything they did had to be cost neutral.

These three teachers refused to be dissuaded by something so minor as having no money, so they came up with a no-cost plan that confronted the way instruction had always been provided by this team. As they talked about their challenge, they acknowledged a unique characteristic of their team. One teacher was especially gifted at teaching math. One loved to teach science and social studies. The third teacher had a passion for teaching language arts. Why not reorganize themselves around these areas of personal strengths? This was currently being done very successfully in a specialized program at a sister school so there was precedent.

These teachers were politically savvy so before they formally presented their plan to the principal, they first drafted a schedule that accommodated the needs of all their children. Considering the myriad of scheduling issues they faced, the very act of working together to create this schedule strengthened their bond.

Next they articulated the potential benefits of this plan and anticipated their principal's inevitable objections. Here are some of the answers they prepared for questions they knew would be asked:

"Why are you proposing this plan?"

"Because too many of our kids aren't proficient, not OK."

"Why did you choose this particular idea?"

"It's already working at the school down the street. It doesn't cost any money. The kids will be getting the best we have to offer. And we're really excited about doing it! Come on, we all know that when a team of teachers is really committed to making an idea successful, they're 90 percent of the way there."

"Don't you think the kids are too young to be switching teachers?"

"No."

The principal agreed to support them, and off they went. We were so proud of these teachers! They understood the TurnAround Schools model for creating exceptional systems, and they have an excellent chance of being successful. Will they be? We don't know because they will begin this intervention when the new school year begins. Really, what's the worst that can happen? At the end of the next school year, they'll revert to their old way of doing business. But if they're successful, which we suspect they will be, they will have found a better way of meeting the needs of all their students, for free.

CLASSROOM INTERVENTIONS

Brilliant teachers intervene in their classrooms every day and never think twice about it. They do so intuitively, and they do so constantly. Carol Adams is one of the best. Carol is a third grade teacher at Los Peñasquitos who never once believed her job was to teach a classroom full of children. She believed her job was to teach each individual child in her classroom. The difference between these two approaches separates average teachers from superstars.

last year Jeff had to intervene between Carol and a specialist who provided services to Emily, one of Carol's struggling students. Carol had dug in her heals. "She can't pull Emily out at 10:45! I don't care if Emily will be in her reading group. I need her here in my reading group! Believe me, Jeff, Emily is making such progress, and I just know she'll be proficient when we do our next assessments. You have to trust me, Jeff. Please let me keep Emily in my group!"

Jeff had learned years ago that once Carol got hold of a kid, she never let go. What could he say? If anyone could work a miracle, it was Carol. He helped negotiate a compromise and Emily stayed with Carol. And surprise, surprise, at the next formal assessment, Emily was proficient.

Carol is a maverick. Every morning, an hour before school begins, Carol and a loyal parent volunteer open her classroom and almost every one of her students shows up an hour early to begin their school day. Carol and this wonderful parent spend that first hour of the day organizing her students into small groups based upon their greatest needs and teaching them. Carol never asked for permission to start school an hour early, and she never seeks recognition of any kind. She just believes that her job is to teach each individual child in the best way she knows how, and she does a masterful job doing so.

What can we learn from Carol? Classroom interventions come in all shapes and sizes. Few can be mandated. Our best teachers see individual children, identify specific needs, think about what will work, decide what they are able to do, and then do it. It's just that simple.

BEHAVIOR INTERVENTIONS

Twelve years ago, behavior at Los Peñasquitos was out of control. Many of the children had little respect for each other or for the adults on campus. They brought with them rules from the street that may have served them well on weekends but which didn't serve them well during the school day. Children were constantly being sent to the office just to sit because their teachers had just had enough, and our overworked secretaries ended up running their own de facto detention. The situation was a mess. Something had to be done.

We approached this problem in our typical manner, and identifying the problem was simple. What proved to be more difficult was avoiding excuses. The first response of several teachers was, "These kids haven't been raised with any manners, and now we're stuck with their disrespectful behavior. We don't get any support from their parents, so what can we do?" No wonder teachers so naturally resorted to punishment. They truly didn't know how else to respond.

As we continued the conversation, it gradually became clear that good behavior for many of our students was a new concept, and that it needed to be taught, without anger and without frustration. We didn't get mad at students when they struggled to grasp certain academic concepts, so why should we be angry when they were still learning to meet our standards of civil behavior? Learning good behavior comes with time, and for almost every student, it eventually did.

Together, we built a common behavior plan that became the standard in every classroom. This plan was created around the six pillars of Character Counts! because we wanted it to have the same positive feel we attempted to create with everything else we did. Each child memorized the six pillars (trustworthiness, fairness, respect, responsibility, caring, and citizenship) and was required to recite them when requested. When a child made a poor decision, the first question was always, "Which character pillar did you violate?"

The plan also had a series of steps that teachers were required to follow before requesting help from the principal. Many teachers didn't realize how completely they had given up their power to teach appropriate behavior when they sent their students to the office at the first sign of trouble. That practice came to an abrupt end with this plan. When a child was sent to the office, he came with a referral that briefly outlined the steps that had already been taken and only then did the principal intervene. If a child showed up without a referral indicating that the teacher had followed the agreed upon steps, the child was returned to class. The few times this happened, the teachers were not happy, but it usually didn't happen a second time. Of course, our teachers always held a "wild card" that they could immediately use in certain serious situations such as children fighting or using profanity toward a teacher.

As a staff, we began to emphasize the teaching of behavior and de-emphasized punishment. We no longer assigned children to detention. Rather, when children were disciplined, they received natural consequences designed to teach appropriate lessons. If they made a mess in the bathroom, they cleaned bathrooms. If they spoke rudely to an adult, they taught a lesson to younger children about their responsibility to be respectful to every adult on campus. If they stole a book, they performed work at minimum wage to repay the school. Even when being disciplined, our children learned important lessons related to their poor judgment.

What happened as a result of these enlightened changes? The culture shifted, and respect became pervasive. When children crossed the street and entered their campus, they knew they were entering a different world. Their faces softened, they relaxed, and they became respectful young people who focused on doing everything they needed to do to be prepared to attend college.

Jeff likens this transformation to Christmas dinner at Nana's house when he was a young boy. Before leaving for Christmas dinner, his mother would gather his brothers and him around her and say, "Don't forget, boys, this is Christmas dinner at Nana's house. It's a very special time. I expect you to be on your best behavior, and I want to see your best table manners." Students now understand that attending school is a similar, almost sacred experience. When they cross the street, it's like going to dinner at Nana's house.

Ten years ago, we had over 500 office referrals that year. Last year in our school of 575 students, we had 86, mostly for minor incidents that occurred during lunch or recess (plus sixteen from Stanley, but he's a special project, and we love him, so we're not counting those!) 86 referrals — that's an average of 2.4 referrals per week, and most of them were for minor deeds.

This shift in culture came with time, but the expectations around behavior can change just as dramatically at your school as they did at ours. All that's required is for you to create your own version of this exceptional system.

COMMUNITY INTERVENTIONS

Every community has resources for helping children that are just waiting to be accessed. Usually, a school doesn't even know these resources exist until a conscious effort is made to find them and then to ask.

In chapter 2 we told the story of approaching the church up the street with a bold offer — we would provide the children and the facilities if they would provide the staffing and the funds to create a state-of-the-art, before and after-school program for our children. That was twelve years ago. Today, this program serves one hundred twenty of our most needy students, and the partnership is stronger than ever. How did this begin? We asked.

Many of our children come from single-parent families, usually moms, and these children can really benefit from adult mentors. We have several adults (properly screened, of course) who serve as mentors to children and who meet with these children weekly. When we see the positive benefits of responsible, stable adults sharing in the lives of some of our children, it warms our hearts. How do we find these terrific mentors? We ask.

Members of a community organization called OASIS, made up of retired (some long retired) men and women, love to come to our school regularly and read with our children. How did we make those arrangements years ago? We asked.

Northrop Grumman Corporation has a large design and assembly facility in the next community, and they send a team of engineers each week to teach science lessons to our fifth grade students. At the end of the school year, they host every fourth and fifth grade student at an all-day, behind-the-scene's tour of their facility, something these children never forget. ("Mr. Lopez!" said one. "Did you know that every engineer had to go to college?") How did we establish this outstanding partnership? We asked.

Interventions are your ace in the hole. They're that twenty-dollar bill you have tucked away in the back of your wallet. They are your academic failsafe measure. When in spite of all your good planning and valiant efforts certain students do not make expected progress, interventions will recalibrate your efforts and naturally get those students back on track.

CHAPTER SUMMARY

Data-Driven Interventions, Both Academic and Social

KEY POINTS

- Well designed and effective interventions are absolutely essential if struggling students are to become academically proficient.

- A staff needs to deliberately and systematically develop their own exceptional system for intervention and then put that system into writing. Remember, even when a system is put into writing, it still needs to be reviewed regularly.

- Current interventions need to be really, honestly, courageously examined to determine if they are effective. Don't fall into the trap of assuming that what should make sense, or what has been done for years, is really working. It may not be. We understand that it is sometimes very difficult for a staff to give up what has been done for years or generations (even if it hasn't worked very well), but that is where strong and supportive leadership plays an essential role.

EPILOGUE

One afternoon while suffering from a foul mood, Damen left his office and walked down the hallway. Ahead of him, walking without apparent purpose, was Travon, a tough ten-year-old boy who had been at the school for about four months. This was the fifth school he had attended, and when he first arrived, Travon wanted nothing to do with the educational seriousness he encountered. But that gradually changed.

Damen, in a voice that betrayed his irritation, hollered, "Travon! Where are you going?" Travon turned around, startled, and instantly replied, "I'm going to college, Mr. Lopez!"

It's because of Travon and all the other Travon's who attend elementary schools across America that we wrote this book. If we waited for Travon's mother to acquire the skills necessary to lift him out of poverty and guide him to success, we'd wait forever, and so would he.

We believe Travon's only hope is for his school to step forward and provide what his mother cannot. At school, Travon will find direction and dream of a future that otherwise would have been denied to him. We know this can be done because schools across America, just like yours, are doing so every day.

If you have courage, and if you care enough for the future of all the disenfranchised children who look to you as a lamp to light their way, you will close the covers of this book, roll up your sleeves, and begin the work of leading your own learning revolution.

We wish you courage, and we wish you success.

APPENDIX A

"We are committed to creating a school that knows no limits to the academic success of each student."

Los Peñasquitos Collaboration Commitment

As staff members at Los Peñasquitos Elementary School, we understand that it is only through effective collaboration that we can develop strategies that result in the greatest academic and social gains for our students. The following are specific collaboration commitments we make as a staff:

Clarity of Purpose: We are driven by one goal, to ensure (at a minimum) that each student is proficient in reading, writing, and mathematics. To make certain that we maintain a laser-like focus on this goal, prior to meetings we create agendas that focus on the academic achievement of children, and then develop action items and agree to hold one other accountable for completing those items.

Respect for Time: We arrive to staff and team meetings on time, and during those meetings we remain focused on the agenda.

Wednesday Team Meetings: Every Wednesday afternoon from 2:15 – 3:40, we work as teams to design instruction and interventions that translate into academic achievement for every child. We agree to hold this time sacred and commit to fully participating in these meetings every week.

Professional Growth: We are open to learning new methods, ideas, and strategies that lead to greater academic success for every child. As one means for doing so, we agree to participate fully in on-site Tuesday Collaboration workshops.

Building Positive Professional Relationships: We are committed to developing strong professional relationships. We will praise one another when we experience success, support one another during challenging times, and confront one another directly and candidly if we have concerns. Additionally, we will celebrate as friends and colleagues outside of school.

APPENDIX B

Tuesday Collaboration Master Schedule

	K/1	2/3	4/5
September	11	18	25
October	9	16	23
Nov/Dec	13	27	4
January	15	22	29

K/1 Tuesday Collaboration Schedule *Contacts: Sara Sumner and Jackie Smyers*	
September 11	**Vertical Articulation** **Topic: Write Source and Lucy Calkins** *(Location: Keri's room)* Teachers will use this time to develop K/1 writing expectations.
October 9	**K Team, First Grade Team** **Topic: Progress Reports** *(Locations: K - Sara's room, 1st - Jackie's room)* We need to review the progress report and agree how we will report student progress based upon our formative assessments. Additionally, we will develop common talking points to be discussed with parents at the upcoming parent-teacher conferences.
November 13	**Vertical Articulation** **Topic: K/1 Behavioral Plan** *(Location: Margaret's room)* Teachers will review our current Responsive Classroom routines and make recommendations for revised routines and/or expectations.
January 15	**K Team, First Grade Team** **Topic: At-Risk Students** *(Locations: K – Keri's room, 1st – Leslie and Dawn's room)* Teachers will review strategies currently in place to support at-risk students, and recommend modified or new strategies.

APPENDIX C

Student Goals Form

My Goals

Student Name: _____

School Year: _____

Subject: _____

My goal for the trimester is: _____

_____

Three things that I can do to help me achieve my goal are:

1. _____

2. _____

3. _____

Parent Signature: _____

Student Signature: _____

Teacher Signature: _____

APPENDIX D

Los Peñasquitos

	September
Kindergarten	• Letter I.D (40) • Phonics Skills (15) • Running Record (1) • Math Skills Checklist (5)
First Grade	• On Demand Writing • Spelling Inventory • Running Record • Math Skills Assessment 1 • DIBELS
Second Grade	• On Demand Writing • Running Record • Spelling Inventory • MAP (Read, Lang, Math) • DIBELS
Third Grade	• On Demand Writing (3) • Spelling Inventory (EWWP) • Spelling No Excuses Words • Everyday Math Beg Assessment • MAP (Read 194, Lang, 194, Math 193) • DIBELS (77) • Running Record
Fourth Grade	• On Demand Writing • Narrative Writing • Everyday Math Beg. Assessment • Spelling — Word Journeys (End 3rd) • MAP (Read, Lang, Math) • DIBELS
Fifth Grade	• On Demand Writing (Persuasive Essay) • Everyday Math Beg. Assessment • Spelling — Word Journeys (End 4th) • MAP (Read, Lang, Math) • DIBELS

*Assessment only given to at-risk students   (#) Grade Level Benchmarks

APPENDIX D

Assessment Plan 2006-2007

February	May
• Letter I.D (52)* • Phonics Skills (21)* • Word Recognition (17)* • Sentence Dictation (18)* • Running Record (2) • Math Skills Checklist (10) • On Demand Writing (8) • DIBELS (LNF: 27, PS 18, NWF 13)	• Letter I.D (52)* • Phonics Skills (26)* • Word Recognition (22)* • Sentence Dictation (22)* • Running Record (4) • Math Skills Assessment (75%) • On Demand Writing (10) • DIBELS (LNF: 40, PS 35, NWF 25)
• On Demand Writing • Spelling Inventory • Running Record • Math Skills Assessment 2 • DIBELS	• On Demand Writing • Spelling Inventory • Running Record • Math Skills Assessment 3 • DIBELS
• On Demand Writing • Running Record • Everyday Math Mid-year • Spelling Inventory • MAP (Read, Lang, Math) • DIBELS*	• On Demand Writing • Running Record • Everyday Math End of Year Assessment • Spelling Inventory • MAP (Read, Lang, Math) • DIBELS*
• On Demand Writing (3) • Spelling Inventory (WWP) • Everyday Math Mid-year (80%) • MAP (Read 200, Lang, 203, Math 200) • DIBELS (92)* • Running Record*	• On Demand Writing (3) • Spelling Inventory (LWWP) • Everyday Math End of Year Assessment (80%) • MAP·(Read 203, Lang, 206, Math 202) • DIBELS (110)* • Running Record*
• On Demand Writing • Everyday Math Mid-year • Spelling — Word Journeys (End 3rd) • MAP (Read, Lang, Math) • DIBELS*	• On Demand Writing • Everyday Math End of Year Assessment • Spelling — Word Journeys • MAP (Read, Lang, Math) • DIBELS
• On Demand Writing (Persuasive Essay) • Everyday Math Mid-year • Spelling — Word Journeys • MAP (Read, Lang, Math) • DIBELS*	• On Demand Writing (Persuasive Essay) • Everyday Math End of Year Assessment • Spelling — Word Journeys • MAP (Read, Lang, Math) • DIBELS*

*Assessment only given to at-risk students   (#) Grade Level Benchmarks

ABOUT THE AUTHORS

Jeff King
Cofounder, TurnAroundSchools

Jeff King first entered a second grade classroom as a new teacher in the Poway Unified School District in1986. Since that time, he has had a broad range of site and district experiences that include:

- Teacher, elementary and middle school
- District Office, technology coordinator
- Assistant principal, Meadowbrook Middle School
- Principal, Los Peñasquitos Elementary School
- Principal, Abraxas Continuation High School
- Principal, Rancho Bernardo High School

Jeff's proudest accomplishments began in 1996 when he was appointed principal at Los Peñasquitos Elementary School. Los Peñasquitos was (and is) a Title 1 school with students speaking 35 languages. For each of the 26 years prior to Jeff's arrival, its students performed at the bottom of the district's 18 elementary schools. Everyone knew it and few cared, because Los Peñasquitos served"those"kids — children who lived in the largest federally subsidized housing complex in north San Diego County.

During the following 12 years, largely under Jeff's leadership, Los Peñasquitos rose from being the school best known for poor student achievement to becoming a national model for Title 1 schools. It earned the California Distinguished School award, the National Blue Ribbon School award, and California's highest recognition for academic achievement (the California 10-10 designation) for 5 out of 6 consecutive years.

In 2006, Jeff co-founded TurnAround Schools. He now dedicates his full time to conducting conferences and workshops that help educators from across our nation learn strategies that enable them to replicate the student success found at Los Peñasquitos Elementary School and other similar high-achieving, high-poverty schools. The strategies that Jeff shares get results. He has the data to prove it. (References are available upon request. Testimonials can be viewed at TurnAroundSchools.com/testimonials.)

If educators in your school or district are open to learning proven, practical strategies that positively impact the student achievement of underrepresented children, please contact Jeff at jeff@TurnAroundSchools.com.

Damen Lopez
Cofounder, TurnAroundSchools

Damen Lopez began his career as a long-term substitute in 1994 at Los Peñasquitos Elementary School in San Diego California. Seven years later, he was named the principal of that same school. Damen's road to the principal's office would include experience as a second grade teacher, fourth grade teacher, and assistant principal of the largest elementary school in the Poway Unified School District. Twice named as both Assistant Principal and Principal of the Year in his district, Damen's success as a leader has helped to showcase Los Peñasquitos Elementary School as an exemplary model for others to follow. During five of the six years that Damen was principal, he and his staff earned the coveted 10-10 ranking by performing within the top ten percent of all schools within the state of California.

In 2004, Damen Lopez founded the No Excuses University Network of Schools. This endeavor helps to build a bridge for all students to attend college as it begins promoting a comprehensive college readiness model starting in kindergarten. After just two years of sharing this message with thousands of educators across the country, there are currently 35 schools participating as part of the No Excuses University revolution. To date this work, which is now influencing the lives of nearly 25,000 students in five different states, has received national attention and has been featured in numerous television and newspaper stories.

In 2006, Damen co-founded TurnAround Schools and now works with schools, districts, and educational organizations throughout the country in an effort to support the development of six exceptional systems that result in academic success for all. Damen's enthusiasm for providing leadership so every student, especially those living in poverty, will be both academically successful and college ready is widely respected. He, along with his staff continue to be honored by the positive changes that schools have made as a result of the lessons learned from the Los Peñasquitos Elementary School story. Damen is available to work with your staff and continues to be inspired by emails from educators from around the United States. Damen can be contacted by emailing him directly at damen@turnaroundschools.com.

ABOUT TURNAROUND SCHOOLS

Jeff King and Damen Lopez founded TurnAround Schools in 2006. Their work is based upon the following two principles:

1. Every child has the right to be prepared to attend college.

2. It is the responsibility of adults in the school to develop exceptional systems that make that dream a reality.

TurnAround Schools organizes institutes where practitioners from remarkable schools share with their colleagues how they coax impressive success from at-risk learners. Principals, teachers, and other leaders leave our institutes with solid strategies they can put into place the following day, and a hopeful optimism for the potential of each of their students.

Jeff King, Damen Lopez, and TurnAround Schools associates also provide personalized, on-site training for schools and districts.

Our mission is to empower educators with proven strategies that get results. We can help your teachers and leaders implement these strategies. We are successful at what we do.

For more information, please visit TurnAroundSchools.com.

For information or to order by mail:

TurnAround Schools Publishing
17265 Prairie Mile Road
Ramona, CA 92065-6412
(760) 788-8725
Inquires@TASPublishing.com
www.TurnAroundSchools.com